TRAVEL RETAIL

THE INSIDER'S GUIDE

KEVIN BROCKLEBANK

ISBN-13: 978-1-3999-3391-9

Cover design by: One Red Kite

Library of Congress Control Number: 2018675309

Printed in the United States of America

For my son, Oliver....

"Strive For Progress, Not Perfection"

- DAVID PERLMUTTER, MD

CONTENTS

WHAT IS TRAVEL RETAIL

Travel Retail refers to restricted locations where access is limited to those who are travelling. It's a fascinating industry which has just celebrated its 75th anniversary in 2022.

The main channels of Travel Retail include:

Airports - this relates to stores within the airside environment (the area after security in most airports). It is the biggest channel for our industry and will be the focus of this section.

Border Stores - this relates to stores at border crossings. Border stores are where people drive or walk across a border and have the opportunity to shop.

Cruise & Ferries - Stores that are on boats or ships. Most cruise ships or ferries will have stores onboard to sell the core categories.

In-Flight - Shopping on board the plane. Most flights have an inflight magazine or an on-screen shop in their inflight entertainment system to enable people to buy on the move.

Diplomatic and Military Stores - These are for use by diplomats or military personal.

Travel Retail is a unique channel. It has its own way of working, its own language and metrics.

The Travel Retail Offer

Travel Retail is usually positioned around 3 key messages:

Savings

Stores in these locations usually have a price saving compared to the high street or downtown stores. These stores are positioned as Tax Free (meaning free of sales tax) or Duty Free (meaning items within the Liquor or Tobacco category are free of government duties).

Exclusivity

These stores may also have exclusive products that cannot be bought anywhere else other than in Travel Retail.

Convenience

These stores may offer product that are not always the cheapest or exclusive but it is convenient to purchase those products while travelling. Examples of this might be headphones, water, toys etc.

Reasons For Shopping

The reasons for shopping can vary but the central themes are:

- For Me (a treaty for myself or a routine purchase)
- For Others (a gift or a request from someone else to purchase a product on their behalf)
- Distress Purchase (must have items that have been taken away (Liquids and Gels) or forgotten).

Zika

"Zika is a mosquito-borne infection caused by Zika virus, a member of the genus flavivirus and family Flaviviridae. Zika virus was first isolated from a monkey in the Zika forest in Uganda in 1947.

Since 2015, an outbreak of Zika virus infection has been occurring in the Caribbean, Central and South America, Oceania (Melanesia, Micronesia and Polynesia) and some parts of Asia." Source www.gov.uk

With the 2016 Olympics, athletes had to decide on whether to compete or not. Zika has an impact on unborn children and can be transmitted in a number of ways. Pregnant women and couples who planned on having children in the following 6 months were advised not to travel.

Epidemics

Epidemics in general have an impact on travel. Viruses such as Avian Flu, Ebola or even Foot & Mouth disease, if not kept in check could spread globally very quickly through air travel.

If you have ever travelled to Hong Kong you will notice people with special thermometer guns to check the temperature of arriving passengers. In such a small, densely populated location such as Hong Kong, a virus can have a devastating impact.

All epidemics will impact travel and therefore spend.

Natural

Weather

The weather is always a factor, particularly when it comes to high-capacity hubs such as Heathrow. A hurricane or a snowstorm can knock out schedules very quickly. Grounded planes have a knock-on impact across the network. If planes cannot take off from an 'at capacity' airport, it means other planes cannot land because there is nowhere to put them.

In situations like this, the short flights are the first to be cancelled to ensure that the long-haul flights that are in the air can land and be taken in.

With modern technology and the introduction of better planes, the routes can be adjusted to bypass poor weather wherever possible during the flight.

In short, if people are not flying, they cannot spend. This is a challenge for airports and retailers alike.

Natural Disasters

Natural events such as the Ash Cloud in Europe or a major earthquake can have a significant impact on flights. This disruption needs to be handled by the retailer and adapted to. Sales are impacted where flights are affected. These types of incidences are beyond the retailer's control.

Security

Terrorism

Airports come under significant pressure when dealing with potential terrorist threats. This increased resource to screen passengers and staff. These systems and processes in place can be an expensive business for airports.. In some major airports like Heathrow, getting staff airside passes can be a challenge. (Authors note : It took me 5 months to get my airside pass). This has significant implications on resource planning, costs and operational efficiency. With the bounce back from covid happening, getting everything back up to speed is dependent on staffing. If it takes weeks and months to get airside passes sorted, it can have an impact on the effectiveness of the airport. There are those who would argue that companies should have been prepared sooner but this is the benefit of hindsight speaking. Everything opened up relatively quickly and there was a high degree of uncertainty as to whether people would travel.

Bomb Scares

Linked to Terrorism, there are the typical bomb scares. This is where calls are received to the airport and the terminal must be cleared. This is incredibly disruptive for all. It means that some passengers are delayed or even worse, some flights are cancelled. If this is the case, the passenger is unlikely to stop and peruse onsite retail stores.

Government Warnings

In today's age, there seems to be an ever-growing list of warnings on destinations to avoid. Tunisia was a good example. Due to the terrorist attack at the beach resort in June 2015, holiday makers stopped travelling to this destination. This had many consequences for the Duty Free retailers both in Tunisia AND in the airports that fly to Tunisia. This also had a devastating effect on tourism for the country.

Security Threat Level

Terrorist attacks and wars place countries under pressure to protect the people. There are various levels of security threat and this can lead to travellers deciding to change their holiday plans. This impacts passenger numbers and therefore revenues for all aviation stakeholders.

Airport Operations

Air Traffic Control Failures

From time to time, air traffic control can have system failures or operational failures that lead to a disruption in flight patterns. This can have an impact on passengers, particularly those transiting. If the amount of time available in the airport is compressed it may remove the opportunity to shop.

Employee Strikes

There is one European nation that is particularly famous for its strikes, particularly when it comes to air traffic control. This causes significant disruption to travellers and has a similar effect to the point above.

Early Call To Gate

For an airport, there is a significant balance to achieve between operational efficiency and revenue generation. You may have already been aware that if a plane is on the ground it becomes a cost rather than a revenue generator. The speed of turnaround is critical as delays by the airline can generate additional fees for the airline amongst other things. An airline will want to get people to the gate and queuing as early as possible. This means that they can load the plane and be ready to depart on time and get their slot on the runway.

Ryanair have been particularly smart with their queuing system. Many times I have headed out to the gate ahead of the gate call (once you take a regular flight you get to know where they will fly from) and I have seen the seating at the gate crowded.

Whilst this is good for the airport and the airline, it is not good for the shops. Minimal dwell time in the airport has a significant impact on the amount of people that spend using low cost carriers.

The bigger the airport, the more likely the passenger is going to be called earlier. If they are not in the main departure area, they have less opportunity to spend.

Computer Errors

In 2017, British Airways had a catastrophic global IT error that left 75,000 people stranded. The crowds at Heathrow made the airport 'look like a refugee camp' according to one airport worker. This level of disruption can cause major issues for retailers and lost sales. Very often, retail staff will be called upon to distribute water, provide assistance and be an extra level of support for the airport.

Cancelled Flights

Cancelled flights are inevitable and this can have an impact on the operations of the retailer. If flights are cancelled and passengers leave the airport, they must have all of their Duty-Free purchases refunded.

Crashes

An air crash can create disruption to the normal operations of an airport and this will lead to a reduction in capacity and this has a knock on effect for the retailer. Thankfully this is a rare event.

Retailer Operations

Sickness & Absence

In a bubble like the airport, sickness and absence can create additional pressures for the retailer. Draughting in support at short notice can lead to significant difficulties. A shift may have to go ahead without the right level of staff and this has an impact on service level delivery, sales and the customer experience.

The retailer will have a limited resource pool to draw from due to the fact that all personnel working in store MUST have an airside pass. Those who have a temporary pass must be accompanied at all times. Once again, this presents a unique challenge for the retailer.

When someone calls in sick, the member of staff covering would need to travel to the airport, park in the car park, get the bus to the terminal, go through security and get their briefing before they hit the shop floor. This is a big chunk of time where the passenger experience is disrupted.

Recruiting

In all businesses, finding the right talent is often a massive challenge. Finding the right frontline teams with the right attitude, aptitude and experience can seem like a mountain that is almost impossible to climb. Add to these challenges that these people need a clean history for the last 5 years and it becomes even more complex.

The right people are hard to find. Our mystery shopping findings have been testament to that.

Travel To Work

Getting the right people to the right place at the right time has always been a challenge. If an airport operator and retailers are to get their teams into the airport ready for the passengers to start arriving, transportation can be an issue. When aligning staff to the right time in Stansted, it meant that staff had to be at the airport for 4am. Public transport does not run at 4am. For people working at the airport but who need public transport this is a problem. For context, 76,000 people work at Heathrow. Living locally might not always be possible.

Airside Passes

Airside passes can seem like they take forever to receive and they can be very expensive to acquire. My pass took 5 months because I had spent a year backpacking around Asia. Those responsible for the airside passes wanted my full history for the previous 5 years. Every country I had been to, the dates, where I had stayed, everything. This can be off-putting for some people applying to the airport.

Shoplifting & Staff Theft

It may come as a surprise but airport retailers also have to manage the challenge of shoplifting. One particular target is Tobacco products. Some airports have organised gangs who purchase low-cost tickets to destinations and hit the stores. The products are then sold on for a profit.

Whilst airside is a controlled environment, it is also a place that can be perfect for shoplifters due to the high volume of passengers.

Another factor to consider is staff thefts. As with all retailers, theft is a common problem and Travel Retail does not escape this. Products taken can then be sold on sites such as Facebook or eBay.

When products such as Tobacco are stolen, the retailer not only loses the stock but they also have to pay the government the lost duty. This means that a stolen 1000 pack of cigarettes ends up costing the retailer a substantial amount of money.

Rules & Regulations

One Bag Rule

Low costs airlines such as Ryanair have famously applied a one bag rule that meant the passengers could only get onboard with a single piece of hand luggage. This presents a challenge for the passenger and of course the retailers. If the passenger has not got enough room in their hand luggage or handbag, this will deter people from shopping.

In most cases, this has been lifted to allow a bag of shopping but this is still an issue that can surface at any time.

Government Tax Rates

Particularly with Duty on Alcohol, changes in Duty can be a complex issue to deal with. This has an impact on the pricing of hundreds of products for the retailer and this needs to be dealt with quickly and efficiently. This can also lead to an impact for brands when prices come under negotiation.

Fire Regulation

Airports have incredibly strict fire regulations. This means that all furniture must be fire resistant for an amount of time before it burns. This is driven by the need for high safety standards in an environment where large volumes of people are. This is particularly challenging when things like Christmas decorations must be fireproof. Contact your retailer or airport to get specific information about fire regulations for that location. If it isn't fire rated, it isn't going in.

Building Regulations

Similar to the problem of Fire Regulations, work within airport comes under strict regulations. Of course this may differ from airport to airport but the principles are the same. There are strict codes of conduct in terms of risk assessment and how work is completed. Simply going in and changing a lightbulb in a store in an airport isn't as straightforward as you might think. There is the safety of the passenger to consider, the equipment that is used and the number of people required to make that lightbulb change happen.

Financial

Exchange Rates

This is a major influence on sales for a travel retailer. Currency fluctuations have an impact on spend but this reaction is likely to be delayed by 2 to 3 months. After the Brexit vote, the pound fell in value. This led to an increase in bookings and for the summer of 2017, inbound travel to the UK increased 18% year on year (Source: Forward Keys).

Travellers take advantage of the cheaper rates and increase their spend.

Brands need to be particularly careful when evaluating the data provided by retailers as this can lead to changes in strategy or erroneous tactics. Always check on currency rates when analysing data.

Recessions

Recessions are always a struggle but on the flip side, people will always travel (when permitted! Covid has taught us that!). During a recession, people become more cautious about spending and may have less disposable income. This is a challenge for all retailers but can be more accentuated for Travel Retail.

Capital Investment

Most concession agreements involve store upgrades and updates. This requires capital investment. Sourcing investment in a tough market may be challenging at times. The return on investment is likely to be of focus. This forces retailers to make decisions about where to put their money in order to get the best return. Competition for funds means that some easy wins are overlooked.

Competitive

Concession Structure

The space allocated to the duty-free retailer in an airport is not locked in. The retailer does not pay rent like a retailer in domestic. Retailers must put forward a bid to the airport at the time the space goes up for tender. The tender is usually based on a percentage of sales and those percentages can vary by category (and in the case of the UK until recently by EU or Non-EU destination sales). There is also a Minimum Annual Guarantee (a MAG) that must be hit. This fee structure ensures that the airport benefits as passenger numbers and therefore sales, increases. The airport also uses the minimum guarantee to protect themselves from underperformance.

If a retailer with a desire to capture a location overbids it can lead to a very difficult situation indeed. If operational costs exceed expectations, margins (that are already thin) can become squeezed. The airport can also push hard in the tender process to a point where the fees become too high. DFS handed back Singapore because they felt that it was no longer commercially viable to have stores in that airport.

Sometimes a retailer might overbid in the hope that they a) become profitable in the later years of the agreement and b) end up having a strong relationship with the airport which locks them in for longer through contract extensions.

It is without question that there will be some retailers that are operating locations at a loss. WDF did a great thing where every location had its own P&L. This led to more efficient operations and resulted in them withdrawing from locations that were clearly making a loss.

Share of Wallet

Share of wallet is a huge challenge for the traditional Duty-Free retailer. This refers to the passenger having a limited amount to spend and therefore having to decide how they are going to spend that limited amount. Who gets the biggest share of their spend?

Remember the days when you might have a Duty-Free shop, a cafe, a book shop and lots of seating? In today's airports, the passenger has far more choice. There is a wide array of Food & Beverage outlets, the Duty Free concession, then a choice of luxury stores and specialist stores such as electrical or jewellery stores. Some of those stores will be run by the master concession but others are not.

With a limited amount of time available and a growing choice of stores and places to eat, the traditional Travel Retail stores are having to compete harder than ever before to drive growth.

Showrooming

Showrooming is where shoppers look at the physical product in store then go out and purchase the product online, often for less than the price of the airport store. This isn't just an airport phenomenon but it operates in a slightly different way than it would in domestic retail. During our observations in a domestic setting, it is usually the lack of service and staff interaction that drives shoppers onto their phones and into the arms of Amazon who will happily help the shopper become informed about the product and sell at a cheaper price.

Online Shopping

Online shopping is big business and it isn't just Amazon who gets the benefit. Other online stores are getting in on the action and this is seen as the beginning of the omni-channel environment - being able to purchase anytime, anywhere and any place.

This is a major threat to Travel Retailers. Shoppers can be watching TV, be using their tablet or phone to surf, see an ad for a perfume and buy on impulse. All this can happen rather than wait to buy it at the airport.

The other danger for brands is that luxury products become commoditised and therefore they reduce in perceived value. Buying a £20 bottle of fragrance is one thing, buying a £300 face cream on impulse via a website? Of course it does happen but the exclusiveness disappears.

Price Comparison Sites

Of course, the previous points do cover price comparisons in one form or another. I want to call out those specific Price Comparison sites that claim to provide the shopper the ability to make an informed decision about the product based on price.

This is a dangerous precedent as this can also end up putting off a shopper entirely. People are curious. Imaging you are flying return from London to Bangkok direct. You find that the product you want is slightly cheaper at your destination. You put off your purchase. You browse further to find that Dubai has the product you need at a slightly cheaper price than the store in Bangkok. What are you going to do? As a traveller you might assume that London and Bangkok are expensive and not shop at all. Dubai is the cheapest but you are not going there.

Some airports stipulate that their airports stores must be the cheapest compared to a competitive set of airports or a set of airports within a region.

There are many reasons why prices may vary on a global scale. This will be covered in more detail at a later stage. This does however put the retailer in a difficult position and it becomes the inevitable race to the bottom. Who can sell the product at the cheapest price?

This is not commercially viable or sustainable. The pressure is then put onto the value chain to drive out every ounce of additional cost. Another example is British supermarkets where competitiveness is all about the efficiency of the distribution channel. Mechanisation (using robots and algorithms) in the supply chain has arrived to deliver every increasing efficiency and reduced costs. Unfortunately supply chain is an increasingly complex area for Travel Retailers and this can be an expensive business.

An example would be that airports charge a fee for every cage to be processed and screened by security. So, that means that every cage filled with product has to be screened by the airport and they charge you for that. This isn't a fee domestic retailers have to pay.

I am sure there are many other factors that spring to mind when you think about airport retail. Indeed, Cruises, Ferries, Border Stores etc. all have their own challenges unique to their channel.

Now that you are aware of some of the challenges that retailers face in this market, it is time to consider the shopper journey.

Summary

Brands may sometimes be frustrated at the level of funding that is required to run promotions, activations and staffing, however, when you consider all of the above, these retailers do not have it easy. It may not change the brands perspective but it should at least increase understanding.

Given so many variables that can have an impact on the channel, it really is a testament to the resilience of the industry and its ability to bounce back. As we have seen though, much of that is down to the willingness and desire that people have to travel. Without those people travelling, we do not have an industry.

Key Learning Points

The key learning points in this section are:

- Travel Retail has a significant amount of challenges
- Covid-19 has shown that even virus can bring the industry to its knees
- Small issues (i.e. staff absence) can have an impact on sales
- Despite all of this, Travel Retail is a resilient industry
- When dealing with retailers, understanding these issues and sensitivities can help create stronger relationships

PART 3

THE SHOPPER JOURNEY

For Travel Retailers, the most important variable in the retail equation is the passenger. The aim of retailers is to get passengers to visit the store and to make a purchase. Unfortunately for the Retailers, the focus for the passenger is to get through the airport and onto a plane.

The key is to understand the shopper journey. Brands and retailers can begin to tailor their offer and marketing in a way that is likely to encourage shoppers into the stores.

The Shopper Journey Stages

Within an airport, our focus groups have shown that the Traveller goes through 5 distinct stages before the board the plane. Those stages are:

- Pre-Airport
- Arrival
- Check in
- Security
- Departures

These stages are all have an impact on the traveller. The traveller will have certain expectations about each stage and will be comparing those expectations with the perceptions they have. Should each stage fall short of their expectations, the experience will be seen as negative. This can lead to the domino effect.

Pre-Airport

This is the stage before arriving at the airport. This can be considered as the point where people start their journey to the airport to arriving on site. Travellers can arrive from the airport in a number of forms including:

- The home
- The office
- A hotel

For some this is an exciting part of the journey, for others it is an obstacle that needs to be overcome. The journey may involve one or more of the following:

- A car journey (self-driven or being driven)
- A train journey
- A bus or coach journey
- An underground / mass transit system

All of the options above come with the possibility of stressors. This is where roadworks, traffic jams, train breakdowns and other inconveniences can have an impact on the traveller. Any part of the journey that goes wrong will make the traveller feel uncomfortable. A smooth journey will, of course, ensure that the traveller arrives with a positive frame of mind.

During this time, the traveller may have time to reflect on or plan their next steps. Will they find where they are going? Are they going to need to eat? Will they pick up a paper or a book? Will they shop etc? Are they meeting anyone?

Whilst this may be a stressful time to some, it is also the beginnings of excitement or even nervous anticipation. Depending on the reason for travelling, they may be relaxing and lowering their inhibitions with regards to spending. Many people save money to spend while on holiday and for a lot of people this will include preparing to spend money at the airport. The reason for travel and the time of travel will influence how people perceive their journey. Will it be excitement? Frustration? Boredom? An example might be those who are flying out to one of the Spanish islands to spend a week in the sun and nightclubs. People have been seen arriving at the airport ready to go straight to a nightclub and the drinking starts early! Will they be excited? Indeed they will!

Arriving

This stage is from the point of arriving on site through to the point where the traveller steps up to the check in queue. This might involve walking from the station into the airport, it might involve parking the car and using the shuttle bus to get to the airport or it may even be a case of navigating the internal network once inside the airport.

Once again, this element of the journey can be stressful. Our research highlights that the passenger has an expectation of seeing staff visible throughout the airport. It was interesting to see that although most people felt that they did not need to speak to the staff, there was a level of assurance and confidence that it gave to know that there was someone to guide them if needed.

Navigation is a critical factor to get right in the airport. Clear, easy to follow signage that makes it simple to find your way around the airport is key to stress reduction. We found that in one airport, in its quest for simplicity in its signage actually caused problems. Our observations showed a number of passengers confused over where they should go. This led to people stood in crowds trying to decipher the signage. Heathrow on the other hand, does navigation very well.

Like anything, Navigation within an airport is easy once you know how. The problem is, every airport can be different. One factor to also consider is that there is a growing number of people who are first time flyers (with reference to the Chinese) and also a large number of passengers that are infrequent flyers. These are the people who struggle to find their way through the process of travelling. These are also the most likely to feel stressed or confused. Once people are in this state of mind, they are less likely to shop.

Check In

This is often an overlooked part of the airport experience however, it is considered to be an important stage in the journey for the traveller. Long queues and rude staff have a major impact on the mood of the traveller.

There is an expectation that the traveller will receive a friendly greeting, be able to communicate all the relevant information they need with a warm smile and a friendly tone. The traveller also does not want to feel rushed as they want to feel like they have all the right information to proceed with their journey. This in itself presents a unique challenge. Travellers do not want to feel rushed but they also do not want to stand waiting for a long time in a queue. This is a challenge for the airports. How do they balance efficient use of staffing and customer expectations?

The introduction of self-check-in and self-bag drop has helped alleviate the queues but this adds an extra dimension to the challenge. The lack of human interaction and assurance can also give the traveller an 'empty' experience. The airports and airlines are also reliant of the ability of the traveller to navigate these systems for themselves. Even as a frequent traveller, I personally have found some systems a little bewildering.

This is the stage that passengers find just as important as the next stage.

Security

Whilst people want to have a quick security experience, they also understand that in today's world, a decent security system is required and therefore will lead to queues. The key here is that passengers EXPECT it, they UNDERSTAND it and will be more tolerant during this phase of the journey. Queues will still lead to frustration but the important thing to remember is that it needs to be managed. If the queue is too long, you anger people.

The key then is to ensure that the security experience meets the passenger expectations. This will not have a detrimental effect on the passenger in terms of shopping.

Where things go wrong is when there is:

- Confusion
- Lack of Direction
- Lack of Interaction

All of these can be avoided by providing people with the right information in a timely manner. Airports are trying to compensate and manage this by putting average walking times on signage to help people manage their time better and avoid stress.

One of the team went on holiday. On their return, they came through airport security and as they were going through, the buzzer went off. They were pulled to one side for further inspection. After an initial discussion, they found that it was just a routine inspection and that the alarm goes off after every X number of passengers. The family proceeded through the airport feeling a little unsettled and realised that they had a bottle of water in their son's bag that the screening had completely missed.

Some people feel affronted by the need to almost strip off when going through security. At the time of writing, a passenger needs to:

- Remove coats and jackets
- Remove watches & belts
- Take computers, tablets and phones out of their cases
- Remove shoes
- Put all liquids and gels into a small clear plastic bag
- Ensure that all liquids and gels are in containers of less than 100ml

Once through security, they need to put all these items back on. All of this takes time to do and everyone feels rushed. The other issue is that there is often not enough space to be able to re-pack quickly and effectively. This puts pressure on the passenger.

Sometimes, it doesn't need to be about shorter or faster queuing times, it can be about a better queuing experience. Free Wi-Fi has certainly helped with distracting the passenger which compresses perceived time in the queue. On the flip side, less time airside means less time shopping and spending.

Departures

Once through security, there are certain things that passengers will go through. These are often referred to as passenger rituals. These include:

- Double check passport, boarding pass, phone and wallet
- Check the Flight Information Screen
- Go to the toilet (99% of people will go to the toilet before they board)
- Buy a coffee and or water

- Purchase a paper or book
- Pick up any distress purchases (this can be defined as forgotten items such as plug adaptors, products to replace those confiscated by security).

It is a sequence that almost all passengers go through in its entirety or in part. All of these elements detract from the main thing all retailers want – for people to shop.

Once these rituals are out of the way, the passenger will explore the options available in the airport. These options will include the core airport shopping offer (Liquor, Tobacco, Confectionery, Beauty, Luxury), Bars, Restaurants and other stores. The other option for travellers is the airline lounges or the seemingly ever-growing number of "pay to access" lounges.

With airports growing and adding more retail options airside, the competition over the share of the passenger's wallet is growing. Passengers today have far more choice than ever before once they reach airside. They can choose to spend their time in café's, having meals, perusing fashion stores or just spending time sat in seating areas waiting.

Traditional tax and duty free stores are having to be more creative to get the passenger to become a shopper and for the shopper to become a buyer.

The Domino Effect

The other challenge that airside retailers have is the domino effect. Whilst leisure travellers are less inhibited when it comes to spending, stress is a key factor that can switch a buyer to a non-buyer very quickly. The problem is, all it takes is a series of small failures to meet expectations during the journey and this would lead to passengers turning into non shoppers.

So what would a series of small failures be like? It's a jam in the ticket machine at the station, it may be a train delay, then a long queue for check in, and finally a rude security guard. It may be enough to make people feel stressed enough not to shop.

Add on other factors such as "call to gate" being early, this impacts dwell time (the amount of time airside) and means that passengers spend less time where they can shop and spend money. This is a particular challenge for low-cost airlines such as Ryanair or EasyJet. These types of passengers see the trip like a bus service, will get to the airport late, know how to navigate their way around the airport to get to the right gate before it is even announced. With such limited dwell time, the prospect of them spending becomes very limited.

What is the Domino Effect?

Children often find Dominoes fascinating. They open the box, tip them out and the first thing they will do with them is put them up on their end to make a trail. Their eyes light up with glee when they knock the first one and it sets off a chain reaction. As each domino falls, it knocks the next one over and so on until all the dominoes have fallen over.

People can be like dominoes when it comes to levels of patience and tolerance levels. Ever had a day where everything seemed to go wrong? It could be something as simple as the alarm not going off, then burning your toast and then realising the top you wanted to wear today is still wet in the washing machine. The day goes on in the same vein until you get to the end of the day and have resorted to a glass of wine in front of the TV.

So, how would you have felt about the top in the washing machine if the missing the alarm and burning the toast had not happened? Each little thing that goes wrong is like a domino. Our tolerance levels reduce with each subsequent event and this influences our perception of the severity. What might just be "one of those things" could be a major disaster by the 5th thing.

The domino effect in business is where minor failures in service levels all build up in incremental stages that ultimately switch people off from shopping. Small sequential fails all lead to a changed attitude in the passenger. Our focus groups and research has highlighted that even the most keen shoppers can be switched off by a stressful experience.

An example of this was when I was travelling to Shenzhen to speak at a conference.

I had planned my journey in advance. I had arranged to take the train to the airport. The morning of my travel, I checked my train times and found that there was repair works being completed. A replacement bus service was in place. If I took the replacement bus service, I would no longer be able to reach the airport in time. I quickly changed my plans, chucked my bag into the car and drove to the airport. I had not had the opportunity to pre-book and so I ended up paying full price for parking.

On arriving at the airport, way finding isn't great. I eventually found where I needed to go, drove up to the top floor of the car park and searched for a space. I eventually found Number 13, an unlucky number in the UK. I got out of the car and there was a puddle that I had not noticed at the rear of the car which soaked my shoes. Marvellous.

I got my bag out and headed for the lift. I waited and waited. Eventually I got my phone out and started responding to emails. Eventually, as I turned to take the stairs the lift arrived. I took the lift to the Departures floor. I went and checked in and headed to security. I eventually got through having had to go back through the gates after taking my shoes off and I was feeling pretty stressed. In terms of my timing I was running a little late and I wanted to visit the Duty Free store.

I put my shoes, belt and jacket back on. I put my computer, tablet and phone back in my bag and went and did the passenger rituals. By that stage, I was fed up. No store visit. All I wanted was a coffee, a sandwich and to make a few calls. I headed to the nearest café. The choice was disappointing (whatever happened to stores and café's being "always ready") and looked unappetising. I selected what I wanted and I decided that I needed to have decaffeinated coffee. I got to the front of the queue and asked for a de-caff coffee. "Sorry, we are all out of de-caff" was the response. Stunned, I asked for a de-caff tea. I got the same response. I turned around and walked out. I left my tray. I wasn't going to buy food that didn't really appeal and a coffee I didn't want.

Frustrated, I sat down and phoned home. I was chatting away and time passed. I glanced the flight screen and the gate had appeared. Still on my call I headed down to the gate. Once there I realised that I had misread the screen and I should be at the other end of the terminal. I turned round and ran back the other way. I had not noticed that someone had spilt a coffee that had not been attended to and almost slipped over. I sprinted through the terminal and just made it to the gate in time.

I boarded the flight and I was pleased to have a few hours to just relax and not think about the awful journey.

On landing, we were put onto busses and headed to the terminal on a journey that seemed we were driving to another country it took so long. We entered the holding area in the terminal and told to wait for our zone to select which security gate to go through. The passengers from the flight waited for about 40 minutes. I asked a member of staff what the holdup was and I was told that it was the screen that was broken and that it didn't really matter which security gate we went through. I was pretty annoyed but headed through to the terminal.

Wandering through, the terminal was crowded. Too crowded. I tried to find a seat and after about 20 minutes I eventually found one. I tried to get onto Wi-Fi to send a couple of emails – it was mission impossible. I tried to visit the toilets and there was a queue. All in all, it wasn't a great experience. I remembered that there was a Starbucks between the two terminals. I headed there (it seemed like a huge walk at the time). I found it and ordered a coffee. I eventually managed to get onto Wi-Fi and I send my emails. I dashed back to my connecting flight and then headed to Hong Kong. Once again, I felt relieved to leave the terminal. I had had enough. I didn't really get to visit the stores although I did manage to get a view of operational capability as I walked past.

In essence, I was a business traveller going through the airports. I am supposedly, (according to some, the key target audience (the business traveller) but the airport experience in both situations was not great. I did not have the opportunity to browse, even though I wanted to.

The return journey was just as bad. When I tried to buy the "guilt purchase" toy for my son (a guilt purchase is the purchase a gift for someone because you feel bad or guilty about being away), the till system wouldn't accept my card. This caused some issues for me. I then had to go and find a cash machine, pay charges and go back. I then called my bank to ask what the problem was and found that it was in fact their till systems that had the errors.

All in all, a poor experience. This was just me though. What would happen if this was 1 person per hour. At an average transaction value of £45, 1 lost person per hour can be an impact of £250k per year (assuming a 15-hour day). Increase that to 1 person lost every 15 minutes and that is £1m lost sales per year per terminal. Across somewhere like Heathrow that is lost sales of £4m per year, just because the passenger journey fell short of expectations. Micro fails as I like to call them can have a massive impact on the bottom line.

The Golden Hour - Fact or Fiction?

You may have read or heard about the "Golden Hour" in Travel Retail. It refers to the hour that passengers have to spend airside between security and the gate. For those who travel regularly, you might begin to question whether the Golden Hour is actually real. Of course, you have passengers who are connecting (through an airport i.e. travelling from Sydney to London via Singapore). These connecting passengers sometimes have more dwell time than most. For those that are starting their journey, the "Golden Hour" for shopping is not what it might seem.

At every course we have delivered and at every workshop we have attended, we do an exercise with the group. We ask people to allocate timings to each stage of the journey. Every time we do that, we get the same results. Try it for yourself now. Allocate the amount of time each stage takes for someone going on a week's holiday based on a typical airport experience. We agree that some airports are quicker or slower than others.

Stage	Minutes
Arriving and Orientating Having parked your car, got off the train or out of a cab, how long does it take to find out where you should check in and get to it?	
Check In How long does it take to check in or do bag drop?	
Security How long does it take to get from check in and through security?	
Rituals How much time should be allocated to Passports, Tickets, Wallet, Toilet, Flight Board Checks, Distress Purchases, Coffee etc	
Call to Gate How many minutes before your flight are you called to gate?	
Time Left 120 minutes - Arriving & Orientating - Check In - Security - Rituals - Call To Gate = This is the time left for shopping including search, select, queue and pay.	

How did you get on? It is surprising when you start and allocate times to each specific stage of the journey. The time used up soon adds up and before you know it you are heading to the gate.

The table below highlights the average times allocated based on the workshops we have run. As mentioned before, these times can vary depending on the format of the airport (I.e. Are the security gates before or after the shops? Is it a low-cost terminal? Is it a major hub or a regional?). There are a whole range of factors that influence the amount of time spent within an airport.

Stage	Minutes
Arriving and Orientating Having parked your car, got off the train or out of a cab, how long does it take to find out where you should check in and get to it?	10 mins
Check In How long does it take to check in or do bag drop?	20 mins
Security How long does it take to get from check in and through security?	20 mins
Rituals How much time should be allocated to Passports, Tickets, Wallet, Toilet, Flight Board Checks, Distress Purchases, Coffee etc	10 mins
Call to Gate How many minutes before your flight are you called to gate?	45 mins
Time Left 120 minutes - Arriving & Orientating - Check In - Security - Rituals - Call To Gate = This is the time left for shopping including search, select, queue and pay.	15 mins

Time (or the perception of time) of course can be distorted. Ever notice how sometimes time can drag while at other times, it seems to fly by. Other factors such as the airline you use can also influence how time is perceived and used. Those travelling on low-cost carriers are likely to feel rushed and therefore time will pass quickly.

To ensure that the maximum amount of dwell time is available to passengers, airport operations should (and usually do) focus on efficiency. This is why self-bag drop has been introduced to enable passengers to take control of the service experience and also reduce queuing times. Less queue's mean more time to spend.

Another thing that airports should over accommodate on is toilets. When almost 99% of people (a fact from when I worked for an airport) will visit the toilet, there needs to be plenty available. Having to queue mean's less time in store and potentially an increase in stress and stress stops people from spending.

Airport operational efficiency is critical. Time focusing on marginal gains (small improvements) is time well spent. The key is to remove as many barriers as possible so that the friction the passenger experiences is minimal.

Reasons for Buying

One dimension regarding the shopper journey is the reason(s) for entering the store and reason(s) for buying. These might be:

Impulse

A great example is where someone has been pushed through a walkthrough store, they spot something that interests them and they decide to purchase on a whim. That person entered the store and had no intention of purchasing. There may be a whole range of things that triggered a purchase. These could be:

- Hunger or thirst
- Remembering a need or a want
- Being nudged by an advert on the way through the airport
- Seeing an offer that is too good to be left behind
- Boredom

Gifting for others

When people travel, they will often buy gifts for others. This might be as a "thank you for having me to stay" or "thank you for looking after my cat". Grandparents will often bring home holiday presents for grandchildren (I.e. A souvenir, a bar of chocolate etc). Whatever the reason, they are trying to choose a present for someone else. The act of giving makes the shopper feel good about themselves too – a side benefit to gift giving.

Self-treating

When people travel for holiday, their inhibitions are often lowered. Walking into the departure lounge is a step away from the worries and troubles of bills, work and other issues. The mentality of "why not, I am on holiday" is ever present. Some passenger groups will often save money to spend at the airport. Where prices are cheaper than the high street the shopper is likely to indulge themselves and buy something a little bit special as a treat. It may be that perfume they wanted but was too expensive or a premium moisturiser or even a nicer bottle of whisky that they would not normally buy for themselves at the supermarket. It often gives them a sense of ability or permission. Given the weight of the justification, the dreaded "buyer's remorse" is also less likely to happen.

Re-stocking / routine purchase

Another reason for purchase is for the person to stock up on what they normally buy. So, if they usually buy CK Eternity and they are somewhere that sells it for lower than their local store, they are likely to be open to purchasing another (even if they do not need it there and then).

Convenience is often an under rated element of Travel Retail. Generally, the stores are beautiful, well ranged and relatively efficient. If a great store experience is right there in front of you, why have the inconvenience of making a trip to a local department store on your return? In some countries, the Travel Retail experience offers something that you just do not get downtown. Shoppers will take advantage of that convenience and experience.

Exploring / Expanding

This is where shoppers might try other products offered by their favourite brands. It gives them the opportunity to see and feel other options that are not necessarily available to them locally. This exploration leads to greater brand awareness but can also, in some cases, enable shoppers to buy something that other people they know do not have. If you have a marketing background, you will know that scarcity is a powerful motivator or driver and this is why Travel Retail Exclusives are often featured or requested by retailers.

The shoppers will browse the categories that instantly appeal. The level of shopper knowledge may vary considerably. Some may:

- Know EXACTLY what they want and will seek it out
- Require advice on what to choose
- Not have a clue what to buy and want to be sold to

It is often difficult to know or even judge what someone might require. For this reason, it is important that the staff on the shop floor at least acknowledge the shopper and ask open questions.

There are other things that can be done to aid the shopper such as the use of clear store layouts, a logical category flow, clear and easy to navigate subcategory segmentation, easy to understand signage and more.

With all this in mind, it is essential to consider the following when addressing the journey into the store:

- Do shoppers have the chance to "decelerate" and take in their new environment?

- Can shoppers see all the categories from the front of the store?
- Are the categories easy to access?
- Are the categories easy to understand?
- Do the category adjacencies make sense?
- Do the brand adjacencies make sense?
- Is it easy to find the till point and pay?
- Is the exit clear to see?
- Are the staff well trained and knowledgeable?

It might be a surprise to see the question about store exit. Having seen many formats of store within airport, one conclusion that needs to be tested is how people feel about large stores. Some of the most successful stores in the channel do not have too much distance between the back of the store and the main footpath through the airport. This may stem back to our 'Hunter / Gatherer' days where going too deep into caves or canyons could spell danger. Logically of course there are no mountain lions or bears to contend with but it would seem that the instinct is still there in one form or another.

The Last 5 Feet (or 1.5m for those who follow metric standards)

A very important part of the shopper journey is the final 5 feet. Once the shopper crosses the threshold of the store, the clock is ticking. The passenger becomes a browser. The store must:

- Have clear sight lines
- Not be congested (with fixtures or staff stood in groups talking)
- Have categories that are easy to find
- Be merchandised in a way that is easy to understand
- Available staff

- Information available about the categories, brands and products

Once those are in place, the Final 5 Feet becomes a critical stage. As the shopper approaches the fixture, they need to see:

- The display is well stocked and that product is available
- The stock has been brought forward (stock is sat at the front of the shelf not at the back)
- The fixture is clean and free from dust or other things such as paperwork etc
- The display is in some sort of logic to enable people to:
  - Find the products they are looking for
  - Make comparisons if necessary
  - Make better decisions

There are all sorts of reasons for entering the store to browse. They may be:

- Killing time
- Moderately interested and may buy if they find the right thing
- Keen buyers who are searching for a specific product
- Avid buyers who will find SOMETHING to buy. They are impulsive and cannot help themselves. These are the types of shoppers that airports like. They sell to themselves.

In e-commerce, the retailers often refer to the final mile (delivery). The final mile is the most expensive part of the distribution chain to serve. Within bricks and mortar retail, it is all about the final 5 feet. This is where you can make or break your sales targets.

Our assessment of retail is clear. Retailers and brands could do better to convert shoppers into buyers. This means using the right:

- Navigation
- Signage

- Brands
- Assortment / Range
- Staff
- Training (Product Knowledge)
- Selling skills

Earlier, I referred to the domino effect – the cumulation of several minor fails (or micro fails as we call them here) resulting in the person not open to shopping and purchasing. A well-trained salesperson can overcome the domino effect; engaging them in conversation, by making them feel like a guest and by making them feel like they have permission to buy.

Where Retail Fails

All the suggestions I have mentioned above seem to be straightforward and logical. Every retailer and brand will set out to deliver on those however, this is not always the case. It is within these final 5 feet that retail often fails. Shoppers often find:

- Barriers to entry into the store
- Confusing displays
- Difficult to find their preferred product
- Multi-sited product
- Staff chatting
- Dirty and dusty displays
- Price tickets missing

Every retailer and brand sets out to create the model shopping environment. Unfortunately, bad habits creep in and complacency takes hold. It takes strong and determined retail managers to ensure that standards remain at the highest levels every single day. There are methods that retailers and brands can employ to ensure that the stores remain 'on-point' and ready to be traded as hard as possible. The methods focus on ensuring consistency:

- Checklists
- Morning briefings
- Store walk rounds with the managers
- Allocating each part of the store to an individual or individuals to maintain and take 'ownership'.
- Store standards manuals (that are used!)
- Store standards competitions
- "Royal Visits" (Directors visits to the store)
- Mobile store standards teams (who visit stores to get them back up to opening standard)
- Standards related incentives and bonuses
- Disciplinary processes relating to store standards

The best option is to instil a shop floor culture of pride in appearance. This means that the team must remain focused on looking their best, operating their best and ensuring that their store is looking its best.

A great retail manager will ensure that the whole team are kept busy – whether that is serving customers, attending to displays or even cleaning. Some managers believe that teams should always be seen to be available and therefore tasks such as shelf cleaning are not considered as important. The problem with that is that staff become bored and when they are bored, they chat and the customer becomes an inconvenient distraction. So many times I have seen staff that are busy cleaning have been approached by eager customers. Those customer's didn't seem to feel confident enough to approach the staff that were chatting.

Creating An Easier Shopping Experience

Deceleration Zone

Leading retailers have a zone at the front of the store that has space for you to slow down in and orientate yourself. When shoppers walk into a store, unless they know exactly where they are going and what they are going there for, they automatically slow down. Some people even come to a full stop. This slight pause or reduction in speed is all about checking out our surroundings and orientating ourselves. As hunter gatherers, it would have been something humans do naturally. Fast forward a few thousand years and we are still doing it in stores.

One of my key learnings when I worked for Dixons Group was that you should always be able to see the back of the store and the location of every category. In some of the largest Duty Free stores, this isn't always possible. You can see this as a good or a bad thing. Walk through stores are known for increasing passenger spend by approximately 10%. Consider IKEA, if you have ever visited an IKEA store, it is very easy to become lost and disorientated if you do not follow the set path through the whole store. This creates a sense of unease and stress. Despite their size, you can feel an impending desire and need to escape. Does that impact spend behaviour? It will depend on the drivers and motivations of the individuals however, stores that become a maze can push people through quicker than retailers might hope for.

Ease of Access

One airport that I find very interesting is Dubai, as the stores are deep enough for a decent number of fixtures but more importantly, you can see to the back wall and instinctively know that you are not going to be 'trapped' in there. It is a 'safe' space to go in, check the thing that caught your eye and come back out again.

Quite often you will see stores that are so keen to get their product in front of the shopper that they actually block the route into the store. I remember walking into a toy store in an airport in Asia and you could barely get through the store if you had your luggage with you. Time and time again, I have seen the benefit of a "less is more" approach.

Another factor that influences a shopper's ability to shop is the amount of replenishment that can happen during busy times. I have been in Duty Free stores that were simply not shoppable because stock was sat on the floor in front of the fixtures. One way to overcome this is to invest in Space Planning and Planogramming (a team who will plan out how the store is used and how the space is allocated both in terms of fixtures and on shelf). This will optimise the assortment and stock levels to ensure that you have adequate stock and replenishment becomes a less frequent task.

A passenger cannot become a shopper if they cannot cross the threshold or access the parts of the store that they need. Make sure walkways are clear, that there is a suitable distance between fixtures and that the front of the store is open and inviting.

Creating Simplicity For The Shopper

I remember my parents being very brand loyal when it came to supermarket shopping. My mum went every Friday to the same place to do the weekly shop. Now, things are different. As a household we have no real loyalty to a given supermarket. It all depends on what we want, where we are at the time and which outlet is nearest. Each chain offers a relatively unique position on food retailing in terms of shopping experience. What I also tend to notice is the that the 'map' is different in each chain. An example of this is the Bread section will be in one part of the store in a Tesco but in a completely different part of the store in a Sainsburys. Knowing where to go for the items you seek presents a challenge.

A frustrating part of food shopping is when they decide to have a relay at a category and subcategory level. THEN things can get very complicated and confusing for the shopper. Recently on a shopping trip in M&S Food for a basket of items, one of the key things I was looking for had been moved. I searched and high and low for it and eventually gave up. I dumped the basket, walked out and took a short walk to the nearby Tesco superstore. I walked in, went straight to the aisle I needed and then straight to the fixture, picked up the item and went on to do the rest of my shop there. Tesco 1, M&S Food, 0.

Now, when it comes to shopping, I can be a little short on patience and so my case of dumping the basket is probably nearer to an extreme reaction however, people will choose to shop elsewhere next time as they want an easy and straightforward shopping experience.

Within Travel Retail, it is very important to ensure that the core categories are easy to find and that the subcategories are easy to navigate within that and not confusing. Would surrounding Vodka with Whisky really make sense? Where possible, make sure that subcategories are placed in line with most people's logic and are logical across core categories (I.e. Champagne and Makeup could be considered as a potential adjacency – please note that you must do the appropriate analysis to confirm this decision. Each location is different and may behave in a different way).

Way Finding The Smart Way

You can create clear routes through the store to ensure smooth traffic flow which is important. You can also use the in-store furniture to influence the path to purchase. This is a form of nudging. Nudging is a subtle form of influencing that encourages people to change their behaviour. Examples appear everywhere, from marketing to building design. The inclusion of a pen in a letter from a charity asking for donations can increase the chances of the recipient donating. Ensuring that people have to walk past the stairs to get to the lift can encourage people to use the stairs more often and therefore influence their wellbeing. This can also be used in retail. In short, you can use the store furniture to influence where people go. The shape of fixtures, the angles they sit at and the level of visibility / exposure that categories have all help influence where people go when they enter the store. You can influence where hot spots and cold spots are, which categories lead into other categories, how people find their way in and out of the store etc. All of this can have a positive impact on the spend behaviour of the shoppers.

Clear Signposting

One way to make sure that the shoppers are able to navigate the store easily is to ensure clear signposting. This might be in the form of marketing point of sale but it brands themselves can be a simple way to indicate the category. If you have a very clear M&M's stand or a Toblerone display, it tells the shopper that this must be the Confectionery area. If Confectionery is what the shopper is looking for, they know that this is the place to go. Even if they are searching for some local and obscure brand, the presence of the larger brand will ensure that the category is found.

Signposting can also be digital. Digital signage can be adapted to show adverts according to time of day and flight schedules. This is about making the category as relevant to the shopper as possible.

By mining transaction data in the right way, you will find the right brands to promote to the right audiences to make a stronger connection. An example of this would be (in locations that still allow it) having Chungwa cigarettes on signage when Chinese passengers are travelling through the airport for key flights and then having the brand change to another brand when the British are travelling. This creates a dynamic look and feel to the store that speaks to the audience.

Making The Decision Easy With Better Merchandising

At the shelf, it is critical that the display is merchandised in a way that makes complete sense. There are times when a shelf looks like it has had a product added when a space has come available. The lack of rationale or logic makes the display confusing. This means that it is difficult for the shopper to make a decision. It must be easy for the shopper.

There are a number of ways that this can be made easier:

- Merchandising by price logic
- Grouping brand families together (and then putting that grouping into a logical order within the brand family)
- Merchandising by type
- Alphabetical order (like Sephora)
- Colour coding

Further detail can be found in the Space Management section of the book.

How you merchandise will depend on how strictly you want your teams to adhere to it. If you have a category with every changing assortment or pricing and merchandising set to a strict price logic then that can lead to a lot of work re-merchandising the shelves and therefore take up valuable time.

When I worked for Dixons Group, everything had to be merchandised in a strict price logic. I have lost count of the number of times I have had to re-merchandise a TV wall in a superstore with only myself and a trusty but wobbly ladder. This was back in the day when TV's had thick glass screens and deep backs. Of course, the Sony TV's were the most expensive and the heaviest which meant that they were always on the top shelf. Thankfully, I never dropped a TV!

Making the decision easier for the shopper with better information

The other thing to consider when helping to make the purchase decision a little easier for the shopper is to have information available. This is something that is often overlooked. It is widely accepted that people shop in Duty Free for gifts, it is therefore reasonable to assume that the person doing the purchasing may not have the knowledge to make an informed decision. Let me share two such examples:

Example 1

A person goes into store and they are looking to buy a bottle of Whisky for a gift. They may not know anything about the category other than – "I know the recipient likes brands X, Y & Z". That person may be spending £50 and will want to be sure that they are making a good decision. When you walk into the Whisky category, how easy is it to find and buy a product if you know nothing about the products? Of course, you could offer samples but if the shopper does not like Whisky, they could be drinking the finest Whisky and not even know it. In the attempt to fill the store space with as many products as possible, point of sale (POS) space is often compromised and effective POS is the key to helping shoppers make an informed choice. Good POS can educate the shopper about the category, the brand and the product.

Example 2

A male shopper heads into the Beauty category to buy a gift for their partner. They might have a slightly better idea of what to buy as they may have looked in their partner's make up bag... then again.... Probably not! In the myriad of brands, categories, subcategories and products, how does that person make a decision? Thankfully the category tends to have beauty consultants available, however, the experience is dependent on service standards. Beauty is also another category that should consider ways of educating the male shopper enough to make an informed decision.

In short, shoppers need to feel confident that they are making the right decision on a product. It does not matter whether the product is for themselves or a gift, they do not want to experience cognitive dissonance or buyer remorse. Buyer's remorse is that little feeling of doubt about the purchase they have made. I am sure everyone has experienced it at one time or another. Should I have bought it? Can I really afford it? Have I bought the right one? Will they like it? Is it really what I expected? The questions that buzz around can be endless sometimes, depending on how involved the purchase was.

Is it easy to pay?

One danger is that till point's or cash desks are too obscured to be able to find. When you do find them, you want to see that the queues are being well managed. Easy to find till points might seem like a foregone conclusion but this often not the case. Small sub stations dotted around the store can often make things difficult. A bank of tills has become more like the norm now in stores and some have a queuing system to ensure that this part of the retail process remains efficient and effective as possible.

Seeing the Customer Through A Different Lens

If you are a fan of crime drama's you will know that detectives are likely to search for 3 things to get a conviction. These 3 things are:

- Means
- Motive
- Opportunity

If we apply this to the retail environment and the "crime' being a shopper making a purchase, we can start to focus in on what really matters. So let's work through this:

Do the shoppers have the MEANS to make a purchase?

In the concept of retail, do people have what it takes to make a purchase? This refers to the financial capability to make the transaction. This covers all aspects such as:

Can the person afford your offer? Is it worth listing a range of £5,000 Whiskies when your passenger base are "Buckets and Spaders" (people going on a family package holiday to Spain, Canaries or the equivalent). Other considerations include:

- How does currency influence sales
- Are they physically able?
- Do they have an awareness or understand allowances?
- Does the single bag rule cause a problem?
- Can they carry it?
- Do they have time to make the purchase?

Motive

One thing I have noticed in retail is that the very best are always considering the motivation of the shopper. What is it that brings them into the store in the first place? Which category and/or brands are they interested in? And Why? Simon Sinek's book "Start With Why" considers the importance of understanding why people buy and this is something we as an industry need to focus on. We need to move away from the standard list of reasons that are used by research agencies (see below) to uncovering real shopper stories. The stories that shoppers tell will uncover the truly relatable elements that other shoppers can connect with.

Standard Reasons For Shopping:

- To buy for themselves
  - As a self-treat
  - Routine
  - Impulse purchase
- To buy for someone else
  - A gift for a friend or relative
  - A formal gift (i.e. for a business person)
- A distress purchase – an immediate and urgent need for an item (i.e paracetamol)

The big question to ask, does the shopper have a strong enough reason to buy *today* from that store? What can be done to ensure they are motivated to make a purchase? Leaving the shopper to their own devices can lead to lost sales as they can talk themselves out of making the purchase that they really want by deciding to "wait for another day".

Compelling reasons to buy are so because they tap directly into the shopper's motivations to purchase. It is often connected to emotions (i.e. status driven, to belong in a group, to have control over something etc). The task of a salesperson in store is to turn motivation into action.

Uncover their motives and get those shoppers spending. In short, you need to create a sense of urgency, a "too good to miss!" offer to drive action.

Opportunity

Does the shopper have the opportunity to buy? That might seem like an unusual question, after all – there is the store, the product, the till point and someone to process it but we need to ensure that all forms of friction (things that stop the shopper from parting with their cash) are out of the way. Some considerations might include:

- Are there staff available to take the money?
- Is there a queue to be served or to pay?

- Do they have enough information to make an informed decision?
- Can they make an informed decision?
- If they are buying a gift, do they know what the person likes?
- Could they find what they were looking for?
- Do you have the brand / product they want and/or need?
- Do their Duty-Free allowances enable them to buy? (i.e. Norwegians have strict allowances on alcohol).

When we look at the shopper from this perspective (Means, Motive & Opportunity) it starts to help you focus on the barriers to purchase and then you can begin to consider the solutions you need to break those barriers down. Currency an issue for a certain audience? Create a targeted offer for that nationality. One Bag Rule an issue? Connect with the airline in question and work with them to create a solution. Passenger going clubbing? Create a playlist on Soundcloud or Spotify that will appeal to your audience.` Create an app that enables you broadcast "music while you travel". Mother's day purchases? Want a gift box to make it all the more special? Done. Some of these might work, some might not. You will never know unless you try things, test them and measure the outcome. Learn and move forward.

The Service Experience

One of the services we offer is Mystery Shopping and there is a good reason for that. Every time I go into a store - from the local independent shop through to a 60,000 square foot mega store, I am constantly reviewing and assessing the in-store experience. Within Travel Retail, I will always go into store to see how the experience stacks up to what I expect should happen. As someone who has managed shop floors for many years, the eye for detail and how a shop should operate on a day-to-day basis is one that may never leave me.

Our Mystery Shopping service is unique. It is a bespoke service that really drives out great insights and clear actions for our clients. It is not a tick box exercise. Our clients receive bespoke comprehensive reports written by seasoned retail professionals who have yet (I am proud to say) to be spotted as a Mystery Shopper.

Over the years, we have experienced a common pattern emerging. Unfortunately, it does not make great reading. This pattern is 2, 5, 25.

The explanation is simple. For every 32 shopping experiences:

Only 2 were exceptional. This means that we had a great experience and would happily buy from that person / store. In one situation, I mystery shopped someone in the Whisky category and they almost convinced me to make a purchase and I rarely drink Whisky.

5 of the shopping experiences would have led to a purchase if I HAD to make a purchase. This means that it might have been a gift or something that I needed for my trip.

Finally, 25 out of the 32 shopping experiences I would have walked away without shopping. That shows you the size of the opportunity available.

These experiences are not limited to the retailer's own team. These scores also happen for Brand Ambassadors and agency staff too.

Some examples of the types of experiences we have had include:

- Staff too interested in talking with each other and not focused on the customer
- Walking away without answering a question from a customer
- Lack of product knowledge
- Ignoring a customer
- Using their phones for social media
- Trading the shopper down.

It isn't all bad though:

I had one salesperson who was so convincing that I almost bought a product that I didn't need or want. People like this are an absolute asset to their employers. Great to see.

I have had someone go the extra mile to make sure I had what I needed prior to my flight. It wasn't a sale but they guided me to the part of the airport that I needed to be in. Sometimes, it isn't just about a sale.

One of my team had the most amazing experience on a beauty counter - to a level where they would pay for that experience. Amazing service.

The key takeaway here is that there is clearly some opportunity to grow sales. Some might refer to this as "the low hanging fruit" - the improvements that are easy to capitalise on with very little extra effort. It is just a case of changing what you do and how you do it - even just slightly. The experience mentioned above with regards to being traded down is a classic example. By just adding a question - "How much are you looking to spend today?" tells the salesperson the level of product that the shopper is looking to buy. Yes, you may have a fabulous product for £50 but if the shopper is prepared to spend £100 - who are you to argue with that? Just take the money!

The Impact

These experiences might seem trivial or may even appear to be the exception but sadly, this is not the case. Mystery Shopping has always been contentious because when retailers do it, they usually use people who are familiar to the shop floor or those on the shop floor are tipped off. Within one retailer there is the stock question that mystery shoppers use (because it is on that good old tick box list) and that is "Where is the cash machine?". As soon as a member of staff heard that question, they knew that the person was a mystery shopper.

I remember when I worked on the front line, other stores would talk to each other and warn each other when they thought a Mystery Shopper was in the area. Immediately the store went into overdrive - cleaning, tidying, being on best behaviour and doing everything by the book. The scores were of course always high. A retailer has 3 choices - believe it, turn a blind eye (ignore it) or address it. Normally they believed the scores but then wonder why the shoppers complain.

In reality, accepting the scores is actually damaging. Imagine you are a retailer and you have a large store serving lots of shoppers. Imagine just 10 customers an hour had a bad experience (based on our numbers it is likely to be far higher) and each customer was prepared to spend up to £100. That is £1,000 an hour that is being lost. If a store is open 15 hours a day that is £15,000 being lost every single day. That is almost £5.5m being lost every year. Roll that across the number of stores in the portfolio and... You can see that it is a problem! OR... A great opportunity.

PART 4

METRICS IN TRAVEL RETAIL

Introducing Metrics

In this section, we look at the most important metric of all, how to calculate it and how to influence it. Finally, we will give you an insight into how travel retailers approach their business using this metric.

What you will find in this section is based on our knowledge of working with Travel Retailers around the world. You will:

- Discover the most important metric
- Learn how to calculate it for yourself
- Identify the drivers that influence that metric
- Work through examples
- See how you can apply this every day

The Most Important Factor in Travel Retail

What is the most important factor is for retailers? Would it be:

- Sales?
- Passenger Numbers?
- Profitability?
- Lower Costs?

The correct answer is Passenger Numbers. Passenger numbers are the lifeblood of any retailer within an airport. Without them, you do not have sales. Covid19 has certainly made this very clear. Yes you could argue that sales, profitability and lower costs are important but without the passenger, you cannot have any of these. Passenger numbers are like fuel. The more passenger numbers you have, the more opportunities you have to sell to them. Below is a typical chart that highlights 2 years of passenger numbers...

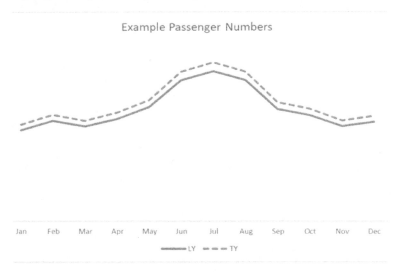

Example Passenger Numbers

Jan Feb Mar Apr May Jun Jul Aug Sep Oct Nov Dec

LY TY

Passenger Numbers

Passenger numbers also have a tendency to fluctuate throughout the year. There are many reasons for this. Some of these reasons include:

- Holidays (I.e. Ramadan, Eid, Chinese New year, Christmas etc.)
- School Holidays
- Events / Incidents (Olympics, 9/11, Sports events etc)
- Seasons (I.e. Summer sun, Winter Sports, Spring Break, Thanks Giving the US etc)

Question

In the example data used in the chart above, we see that June / July / August is a key period for travelling. Why might this be the case?

Hint : what happens to schools during this time?

Not All Passengers Are Equal

To complicate things a little, all passengers are not equal. They behave and spend in very different ways. Think for a moment why this statement is true. What are the reasons for passengers not being equal?

Passengers within an airport environment are made up of a mix of different nationalities, backgrounds and reasons for travel. This makes each airport its own unique microclimate and therefore should be treated in isolation initially. For example, London Heathrow is a very different passenger profile to that of London Gatwick. The two airports are only 40 miles apart but serve different markets.

Some of the factors that can influence the quality of the passengers include:

- Nationality
- Strength of Currency
- Choice of carrier (low-cost carrier (I.e. EasyJet, Ryanair) vs full service carrier (I.e. British Airways, United etc))
- Destination (where are the passengers travelling to?)
- Income levels
- Reasons for Travel (commuting vs leisure)
- Understanding of and attitudes towards duty free

Can you think of more?

So, if an airport is made up of business travellers who commute via a Low-Cost Carrier, it is likely to be a different quality of passenger to an airport where the majority of flights are long haul using full-service carriers that are taking people to premium holiday destinations.

Please note: when we refer to the quality of passengers it really means the propensity or likelihood that they will spend in airport shops.

Why is Destination Important?

Destination is a key factor that is overlooked within Travel Retail. Imagine for a moment, 3 different groups of passengers:

The Smiths

Destination: Benidorm
Accommodation: Large beach side hotel with a large pool
Flights: Included in the holiday package

The Jones'

Destination: Disney World, Orlando
Accommodation: Luxury Villa
Flights: Business Class flights

Post Exam Group

Destination: Party Island
Accommodation: Bargain hotel - lots of drinking, no sleeping!
Flights: Low Cost Carrier

Questions

Do you think these groups have the same brand preferences? The same disposable income? What types of products or brands do you think might interest them?

Often, Destination can say a lot about the traveller. When retailers start looking into purchasing behaviours by Destination, they begin to see patterns emerging (Voyager by One Red Kite allows retailers to build optimised assortments based on the analysis of nationality or destination spend behaviours). This enables the retailer to begin effectively targeting passengers and shoppers in the right way to grow sales.

Question

Write down a few ideas on the following questions:

- In what way could you use this type of information?
- How would it help you make better decisions and increase your return on investment?

Key Learning Points

The key learning points in this section are:

- Passenger numbers are critical for all travel retailers
- Passenger numbers can be affected by seasonality
- Passengers are not the equal (They spend differently)
- Each location is often like a unique micro climate
- There are many factors that affect passengers ability to spend
- Destination targeting delivers benefits for retailers and brands

The Most Important Metric

Earlier we touched on the fact that passenger numbers were critical to the success of a Travel Retailer. As long as passenger numbers keep growing, in theory, so will sales. When retailers tender for airports, they factor the passenger number growth into their proposals.

Previously, we saw this chart:

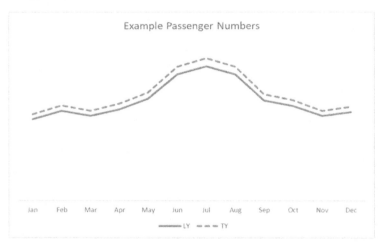

We can see that there is seasonality within the passenger numbers (June to August). Let us now look at the Sales behaviour.

In the sales chart below, we see a different line shape that peaks in March and September. This is a different shape to the passenger numbers chart.

Sales

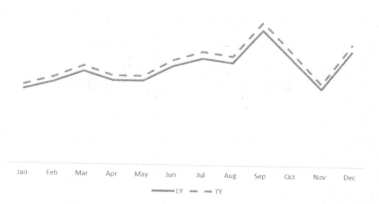

Jan Feb Mar Apr May Jun Jul Aug Sep Oct Nov Dec

━━━ LY ━ ━ TY

We have established that the 2 charts (Passenger and Sales for the same location) follow different lines. To make the comparison easier to see, we can overlay the passenger numbers and the sales together in a single chart.

Pax Vs Sales

Jan Feb Mar Apr May Jun Jul Aug Sep Oct Nov Dec

━━━ Sales ━ ━ Pax

In the passenger number line we see that there is a big uplift in passengers during the summer months. The sales, however, see peaks in March and September.

Question

Why might passenger numbers peak during the summer but sales do not?

To gain a better understanding of what is going on, we need to complete a simple step. We need to apply a metric.

The Focus Of Every Travel Retailer Is Spend Per Head

This is sometimes referred to as Passenger Average Spend, Spend Per Pax or Spend Per Passenger. In this book, it will be referred to as Spend Per Head.

Spend Per Head is a simple calculation but it is a very powerful. It forms the basis of everything that the retailer does. Retailers use Spend Per Head to:

- Understand their sales
- Understand their promotional performance
- Forecast Sales
- Forecast Costs and Budgets
- Create business cases for future investments
- Make decisions on tenders
- Drive and manage team performance

Calculating Spend Per Head

Calculating Spend Per Head is relatively straight forward. The following formula is used:

$$\frac{\text{TOTAL SALES}}{\text{TOTAL MATCHING PASSENGERS}} = \text{SPEND PER HEAD}$$

What are Matching Passenger Numbers?

If the store is in the departure lounge, you will want to ensure that the passenger numbers you use refer to departing passengers. If the store is an arrival store, you will want to use arriving passengers. The key is not to use Total Passengers (Arrival plus Departing). If you only have Total Passenger numbers, divide the total by 2 to give you Outbound and Inbound passengers.

e.g. If Total Passengers for January are 1,000,000 it is reasonable to assume that departing passengers will be 500,000. This is the Total Passengers (1,000,000) divided by two.

Applying Spend Per Head

We can apply the calculation to our example data to create a chart that highlights the Spend Per Head across the year.

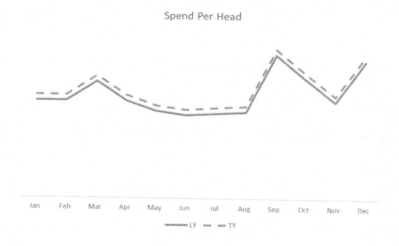

Spend Per Head

Jan Feb Mar Apr May Jun Jul Aug Sep Oct Nov Dec

—— LY — — TY

In this example, we can see that SPH closely follows the same path year on year. In it, where we see year on year sales growth between April and August in the sales chart, that growth is not evident in the Spend Per Head chart.

When we overlay passenger numbers and SPH onto one chart, we get the following:

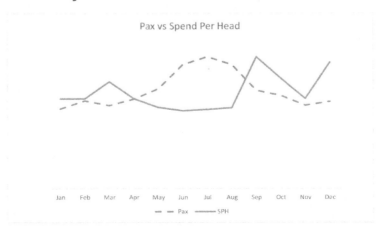

There are 3 things to spot here:

- Spend Per Head actually falls in the summer months
- When passenger numbers fell in March, Spend Per Head went up
- Spend Per Head Peaks in December

So let's tackle these points:

Spend Per Head actually falls in the summer months

If people are going on holiday, it would seem probable that they would shop. So why would Spend Per Head be lower? Well, think about the people who are travelling. There is likely to be a greater number of children travelling due to the school holidays. These all count as passenger numbers. Unfortunately for retailers, children are not able to buy!

Passengers Fell, Spend Per Head went up

This could be driven by a number of reasons including better service standards during quieter times, different passenger types, differing reasons for travel etc.

Spend Per Head Peaks in December

In this location, it is likely that there is greater propensity to spend during the Christmas period. Passengers therefore spend more money in December for self-treat and gifting reasons.

Key Learning Points

The key learning points in this section are:

- Passenger numbers are important
- Sales do not always follow the passenger number trend
- Spend Per Head (SPH) is a key metric
- Retailers use SPH in a wide number of scenarios
- There are reasons for Spend Per Head to fall when passenger numbers are going up.

The Building Blocks of Retail

Successful retail is all about matching products with people. It is about finding out what people want, sourcing it and then selling it to them in a profitable way. All too often retailers (particularly in the domestic markets) will buy product and then try and work out how to sell it to the people that are passing through their stores.

A truly agile travel retailer will adapt their assortment of products to the needs of the local market. This will bring new types of shopper into the store, convince shoppers to buy and encourage them to spend more. This will increase sales year on year.

Of course, sales will go up and down year on year as well. But what is it that REALLY drives that change in performance?

The Key Drivers

Within Travel Retail, changes in sales performances can be broken down into 4 key drivers. Everything stems from that. Understand these key drivers and you can optimise your business with absolute clarity.

These four drivers are:

- Passenger Numbers
- Conversion
- Number of Items in the basket
- Average price per item in the basket

Let's go into these in a little more detail:

Passenger Numbers

This is the biggest driver of sales. Passenger numbers are the number of potential shoppers available. As passenger numbers increase, sales will often go up, but not always. We might hear about how sales increase by +5% and passenger numbers are also rising by +5%. Sales have increased in line with passenger numbers.

Passenger numbers are outside of our control. The only thing that can be worked on is increasing "Dwell Time". The longer people have in Departures, the greater the chance they will buy.

The only thing you can do is to influence the time they have in store. Retailers are getting creative with the introduction of things such as bar's (alcoholic), brow bars, nail bars and interactive zones. Apple stores are very good at getting people into the store and staying in the store.

Conversion

This is the percentage of people that convert into shoppers. This sometimes referred to as penetration. This term can lead to confusion as some refer to Penetration as the number of people who cross the threshold and enter the store. If you are unsure when a stakeholder refers to this term, ask them to confirm. They will be pleased to do so.

The better a retailer does at converting shoppers, the more their sales go up. This is expressed as a percentage:

$$\frac{\text{NUMBER OF TRANSACTIONS}}{\text{TOTAL MATCHING PASSENGERS}} = \text{CONVERSION}$$

(% OF PEOPLE WHO HAVE PURCHASED)

A retailer will do a number of things to try and increase conversion including:

- Create promotional sites
- Create pop-up areas
- Drive the salespeople to talk to more shoppers etc
- Invest in sales training
- Invest in product knowledge training

Units Per Basket

Once you have a shopper who has chosen something to buy, the next step is to get people to pick up more items and put them in the basket. This can be a challenge with a category like Liquor or Tobacco where there is a restriction on how much can be purchased. This is why a holistic view (thinking about all categories) needs to be considered.

A retailer will do a number of things to increase the Units Per Basket including:

- Strategically place shopping baskets in the store
- Add impulse items at the till

- Use Active Selling and Cross Selling
- Use Promotions (multi buy offers)

Question

What else can be done to increase the number of items in the shoppers basket?

Average Price Per Item

The average price of an item often increases naturally thanks to inflation. If inflation is at +2% and sales are +2% (with passenger numbers, conversion and items per basket being the same), in real terms, sales have not moved forward.

To influence this metric, get people to buy a higher price item. This means that the shopper might choose a more expensive bottle of perfume over an entry level price point or by encouraging people to go from Brand X to Brand Y.

Question

How could you get people to trade up in your category? What steps could you take?

The Building Blocks

Now that we have these 4 elements in place (Passenger Numbers, Conversion, Units Per Basket and Average Price), you can start to consider them like building blocks. Everything in Travel Retail sales can be derived from these 4 base elements.

Every action, decision or step should ask "How will this influence the 4 key elements / building blocks?"

Let's work from the ground up....

If you consider Passenger Numbers and Conversion together, you end up with the Number of Transactions. Let's take a look...

Question

If you have 100,000 passenger and a conversion of 15%, how many transactions do you have?

15% of 100,000 passengers is 15,000 transactions. Increase your conversion by 1% point (an extra buyer in every 100 passengers and you would be increasing your transactions to 16,000.

Just 1 more buyer in every 100 shoppers can make a big difference.

Next, if we look at Units Per Basket and multiply that with Average Price Per Item, you get Average Transaction Value.

Question

If I have 2 items in my basket and the average price for each item is $25, how much is the transaction value?

2 items at $25 = $50. If you can get a shopper to trade up, you increase the Average Transaction Value and therefore grow sales.

We can look at this in a visual way. Below is what we refer to as the sales tree.

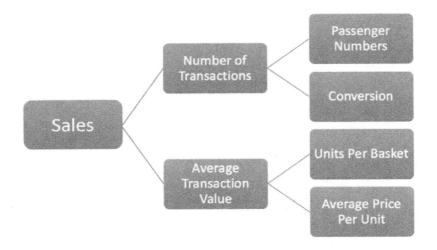

Year On Year sales will be a result of:

- More or less transactions
- Higher or lower average transaction value

The Number Of Transactions will be influenced by:

- The number of passengers going through the airport
- The percentage of passengers you manage to convert

The Average Transaction Value will be influenced by:

- The number of items in the basket
- The average price of the items in the basket

If you can master this sales tree, you will transform your approach to Travel Retail and significantly increase your return on investment. A deep understanding the sales tree holds the key to Travel Retail growth.

Key Learning Points

The key learning points in this section are:

- There are 4 key drivers of retail sales in Travel Retail
  - Passenger Numbers
  - Conversion
  - Average Units Per Basket
  - Average Price Per Unit
- Dwell Time is the amount of time a person spends in the departure lounge
- Encouraging people to spend more time in store will encourage people to spend more.

In the previous section we also introduced the sales tree.

We also touched on the point of passenger numbers. Passenger numbers are outside of a retailer or a brand's control. A retailer cannot get more traffic into an airport. It is outside their circle of influence.

If we take out passenger numbers, it leaves us with 3 remaining drivers of retail sales that CAN be influenced. This is Conversion, Units Per Basket and Average Price Per Unit.

Remember how we calculate Spend Per Head?

This calculation takes away the effect of passenger numbers to leave us with an average spend per passenger which we refer to as Spend Per Head.

Spend Per Head then is influenced by 3 of the 4 key factors:

- Conversion
- Units Per Basket
- Average Price Per Unit

There is an alternative way to look at the sales tree and it is as follows:

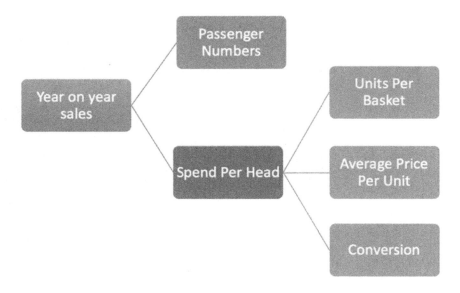

Year on year sales will be the result of changes in passenger numbers or changes in Spend Per Head. Spend per head is the result of changes in the 3 drivers mentioned above.

The Interdependencies

It is worth noting at this point that there are interdependencies to consider. Changing one of the 3 elements might have an impact on the other 2.

For example, you offer 50% off on a product. It is likely to:

- Increase conversion
- Increase the average number of units per basket.
- Reduce the average price per item

Whilst cash has been lost due to the discount, there is likely to be a gain from increased conversion and the increased number of units purchased. Retailers want to increase sales. Dropping the price by

50% will need to either double the number of shoppers buying or get the existing buyers to buy more. Ideally, you would see both (more shoppers, buying more). If it does not do this, it costs the retailer money in sales and of course profitability. Sometimes promotions do not work and losing money is a real possibility.

Another example to consider is how impulse items affect this dynamic. So, imagine that a typical basket has 1 item of Liquor in it at £30. If you run a promotion that gives a discounted bar of chocolate in for £1, it has consequences on the metrics. Such a promotion isn't likely to increase conversion but it will increase the number of items in the basket if most people take it up. The Average Price Per Unit drops significantly. On an individual basis, we see that Average Price Per unit goes from £30 to £15.50 when the bar of chocolate is added. Does that mean it is a negative? Not at all, there are calculations that can be done to evaluate the cash impact of an extra item in the basket. Anything that adds more items into the transaction can only be good thing.

Another example is where you increase the price by +20%. It may reduce conversion and or reduce the number of items people buy but the average price would increase.

One more example - increasing conversion by having more trained staff available might influence people to buy more items and trade up.

With the right information, these changes can be charted. In the waterfall chart below, we see the effect that a discount might have on sales. Sales have increased year on year.

Example Chart To Show The Effect A Discount Might Have

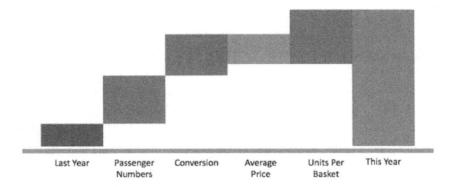

| Last Year | Passenger Numbers | Conversion | Average Price | Units Per Basket | This Year |

In the above chart, we see that growth has been driven by increased passenger numbers, improved conversion and an increase in units per basket. Average price is negative as this has seen a decline year on year.

So, overall there is a net gain. The increase in Conversion and Units Per Basket is enough to offset the decrease caused by the price reductions.

In this scenario, the retailer has sacrificed sales value due to lowering the price.

Is There a Sacrifice?

When we refer to sacrifice, we are talking about the losses you are likely to incur as a result of an action. Here are some examples:

- Are you prepared to lose sales value by discounting? Will the uplift of increased conversion deliver a growth overall?
- Are you prepared to lose shoppers (conversion) or units if you premiumise?
- Are you prepared to lose shoppers by only offering bundles of products?

Sometimes it is ok to lose cash by discounting because the volume uplifts will more than offset the loss.

Premiumisation

Over the last 10 years or so, the channel has pushed to premiumise the stores. The logic was as follows:

Why sell 5 bags of sweets when I can sell one bottle of premium spirits?

Well, there is a point there. Now that we have looked at the sales tree and the components of Spend Per Head, it might be useful to take an alternative view.

Question

With your new knowledge of Spend Per Head in mind, what is wrong with the above statement regarding the preference to sell spirits over sweets?

Key Learning Points

The key learning points in this section are:

- It is possible to influence 3 out of 4 key elements of retail sales including:
    - Conversion
    - Units Per Basket
    - Price Per Unit
- The 3 elements are interdependent (I.e. Reducing price may affect conversion and units per basket).

Influencing Spend Per Head

Let's revisit the following statement and consider why this might be incorrect:

> ### Why sell 5 bags of sweets when I can sell 1 bottle of premium spirits?

By now, your knowledge of the most important metric, Spend Per Head, should help to call this statement into question. The questions you are probably asking now are:

- Would a Whisky shopper put down a bottle of Whisky and purchase a bag of sweets instead?

Probably not!! The Whisky shopper is unlikely to substitute a premium bottle of spirits with a bag of sweets.

- Would the space taken up by sweets be better used for an existing premium category such as Liquor? Or Beauty?

Possibly not. Remember, a multi category retailer needs to appeal to the broadest possible audience.

In the following diagram, we can see that there are Spirits Shoppers only and Sweets Shoppers only. However, where the Venn diagram overlaps, that shows the group of people that buy both.

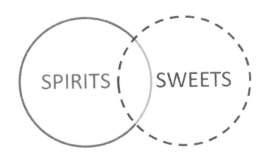

By removing the opportunity to buy sweets, you are excluding a group of shoppers AND you are losing the opportunity for shoppers to buy both. If you have access to the right information, you can quantify this impact in cash terms.

Question

What is the effect of a Whisky shopper who also goes on to buy Sweets on impulse?

Remember the 3 elements that influence Spend Per Head?

- Conversion
- Average Price Per Unit
- Average Units Per Basket

(Yes – I know I am repeating this a lot.... But it is important)

When a Spirits buyer buys Sweets on an impulse, they are putting more items into their basket. This therefore increases Average Transaction Value and therefore Spend Per Head.

The million dollar question therefore is "Which came first?" (a not unlike the "chicken and the egg"). Did the shopper come in for Whisky and then buy a bar of chocolate? Or did someone come in to buy a bar of chocolate and walk out with a bottle of Whisky too? We cannot be sure for certain but we CAN make some educated guesses.

Once again, with the right information, you can make an educated judgement on which indeed came first and therefore make decisions about how to merchandise in the store. The latest analysis techniques we have been using on live projects enables us to have a clearer idea of which comes first in this transaction.

Would extra space to Liquor bring in a different shopper type?

To answer this, we would need to understand whether the extra space would draw in new customers (I.e. With a new sub-category or new brands). Given the broad nature of the Confectionery category, this has the potential to be a compelling offer.

Activations

An activation is an activity that runs in a store. It is usually at a promotional site within the store or at the front of the store. In some circumstances, it may even be a pop-up shop outside the main store.

There are a number of reasons why you might want to run an activation in store:

- Drive volumes
- Drive cash sales
- Create brand awareness
- Launch a new product

The key question should be "what are you trying to achieve?"

Is the activation going to:

- Convert more shoppers (people who would not have bought before)?
- Get more people to trade up (from an existing preferred product or competitor product)?
- Get people to add the item to their basket on impulse?
- Create brand awareness?

An example of an activation comes from the domestic market. We were in Manchester doing some Christmas shopping. We sat in a cafe in a department store having a cup of tea and we could see someone selling a bottle of wine. The bottle looked like every other bottle but then it was given a brief shake and the liquid turned opaque and started swirling like storm clouds. Neat party trick! We did not intend to buy that wine, it couldn't have been further from our thoughts... But we bought one. For context, we were going to go to a dinner party the following week and bought it as a gift for the host. It became a talking point at the party. We were not buying wine, we were buying it for the purpose we intended.... To bring amazement to our host and other guests.

Key Learning Points

The key learning points in this section are:

- Each category has a role to play
- Categories can complement each other
- Activations should have clear commercial reasons for running

Working With Limited Data

If you work within Travel Retail, you will know that data within our channel can often be limited. Retailers rarely give out details such as Transaction Counts meaning that it is difficult to get the measurements we have learned so far such as Conversion and Units Per Basket.

You ARE likely to have Sell Out data (this is the number of units and sales value of your products) of the products your brand has sold. You may even have category percentage uplifts too. If this is the case, you need to apply logic to the problem.

Imagine the following scenario:

Description	YoY
Spirit Brand X Sales	+6%
Spirit Brand X Units	+3%
Category	+5%
Passengers	+5%

In the table above we can see:

- Passenger Numbers have risen by +5% year on year. The category has risen by +5% meaning that the Spend Per Head for the category will be flat (+0%).
- Brand X sales are +6%. This means that Brand X's sales are greater than the passenger number increase.
- Brand X Spend Per Head has therefore increased year on year. (If Brand X sales are +6% and passengers are +5%, it must mean that SPH has increased.
- Brand X has outperformed the category in sales terms (+6% vs +5%).
- Brand X outperformance will mean that they have gained market share.
- Brand X units are only +3%. To achieve +6% sales the average price must have gone up. This is either through price increases or trading up.
- If inflation is greater than +0% year on year, the category sales will have declined in real terms.

Now we need to make some assumptions.

Let us assume that Spirits are most likely to be bought as a single item in this location (I.e. The shopper is unlikely to buy 2 bottles of the same product due to customs allowances).

From this assumption we can now determine the number of transactions that contain Spirits.

With Units at +3% and assuming that there will be one unit per transaction, the number of transactions have grown slower than the number of passengers. (Units (or as we are now assuming Transactions) is at +3% and passengers are +5%). This means that conversion has fallen.

When we combine all of the information, what do we know?

- Brand X Spend Per Head has grown
- Spend Per Head as a metric is driven by Conversion, Price and Units Per Basket
- We can assume that Units Per Basket remains flat (1 bottle per transaction)
- In this scenario, Conversion has fallen
- This leaves Price as the key driver of the growth

This leaves the key questions:

- Have prices in general increased?
- Have people traded up?
- What should you do about it?
- What are the next actions?

This is where you would now need to investigate at a product level within your own brand performance to gain an understanding of what is happening.

As an additional point, brands can often see significant fluctuations in sales that vary significantly from the category performance. See the table below. With the learnings from the previous examples, what can we determine from the numbers below?

Description	YoY
Spirit Brand X Sales	+26%
Spirit Brand X Units	+27%
Category	+3%
Passengers	+6%

Answer the questions below and make a note of your answers before moving on.

- Which has performed better? The brand or the Category?
- Has the Category Spend Per Head increased year on year?
- Has the brand Spend Per Head increased year on year?
- What has happened to price point?
- Assuming one bottle per transaction, what has happened to brand conversion?
- Should the brand celebrate or be concerned?
- What might the retailer response be to your performance?

So let us walk through the questions.

Which has performed better? The brand or the Category?

Well, performance of the brand is +26% compared to the category at +3% is the brand has far outperformed the category.

Has the Category Spend Per Head increased year on year?

No. With Passenger numbers +6% and Category Sales at +3%, Spend Per Head will have gone down year on year.

Has the Brand Spend Per Head increased year on year?

Yes. This has gone up significantly. This may be driven by a promotion or the brand may be on trend. Also, it could be that they are working on a small base (I.e. Moving from $1,000 to $2,000 is a 100% uplift but it isn't a big number if the share of sales is low).

What happened to the price point?

Unit sales are +27% and sales are +26%. This means that Average price saw a slight decline. The question here is, "was this a general decline or is something going on at a SKU level?"

Assuming 1 bottle per transaction, what has happened to conversion?

As units are +27% and passengers are +6%, it would suggest that conversion has increased.

Should the brand celebrate or be concerned?

The brand is likely to celebrate BUT caution is advised. Let's think about what this is really saying:

- *Brand Spend Per Head is up*
- *Category Spend Per Head is down*
- *Brand X has gained significant share*
- *Brand X has therefore STOLEN share rather than grow the category*

What might the retailer response be?

The buyer response could be something along the lines of:

"It is great to see your brand growing so well but it has done nothing to support the growth of the category. In fact you have stolen share from a more profitable brand that we stock. This means that we are being hit twice. Sales are below last year AND the sales we do have are now making us less cash margin compared to what we would have sold with your competitor brand. What are you going to do to help us get back to where we were in cash margin terms?"

Time to re-think the party? Maybe!

So let's just recap this scenario:

- The brand has outperformed the category (SPH has increased for the brand but decreased for the category)
- The brand has stolen share from other brands rather than grow the category
- The brand price point has declined slightly
- Units per basket we assume will stay at 1 bottle per transaction
- This suggest that conversion is the key driver for the brand and the brand is attracting and converting more shoppers.

Keep Asking Questions

In your discussions with the retailer you can ask questions such as:

- So what is the reason for the decline in category spend per head?
- Have prices fallen and shoppers are not responding?
- Have prices risen and shoppers are buying less?
- What has happened to conversion?
- Are people buying into other categories instead?
- What is happening to the total store performance?
- Could we do a category project for you?

A Note About Assumptions

It is absolutely right to use assumptions when reviewing performances as long as you state what they are. If your assumptions are incorrect the retailer or brand will correct you. If they do correct you, it opens up the conversation. Conversations lead to better information and insights.

The same applies to passenger numbers. You use the numbers on websites, from the airports or if the retailers share them.

Key Learning Points

The key learning points in this section are:

- Even when there is limited data, you can uncover a story.
- It is ok to make assumptions as long as you communicate them.
- Stealing share is ok(ish) when the category is performing well.
- Stealing share when the category is under performing can lead to challenge.

Applying What Has Been Learned In A Real-Life Context

There are many ways the learnings within this part of the book can be applied on a day-to-day basis and when talking with retailers. Here are some examples:

"This type of promotion has been shown to drive footfall into the category. More shoppers mean that the category benefits from increased conversion and therefore increasing Spend Per Head."

"This type of activity increases the number of items in the shopper's basket leading to an increasing in Spend Per Head".

"This product appeals to the impulsive part of the shopper and they add it to their basket leading to an increase in Spend Per Head, growing sales".

"This product is a great sell up from our entry level line. If X% of our regular shoppers trade up to this product, it will lead to an increase in Spend Per Head".

"This product (pink champagne) has a core market but is also likely to appeal to Cosmetics buyers. This increases the shopper's basket size and therefore transaction value. The result is cross category purchases and increase in Spend Per Head".

"This product would be unique to your assortment meaning it will bring a new type of shopper into the store. This benefits you in 2 ways. You can target existing shoppers (and grow the basket size) and appeal to a new market (grow conversion). Remember, people who come in for our category may go on to buy other core categories such as X, Y or Z. All of this will help you grow Spend Per Head and increase sales above and beyond passenger growth".

"Male shoppers often find it difficult to choose the right fragrance for a loved one. This new execution makes it easier to do. This means you will be able to convert more shoppers leading to a growth in Spend Per Head".

"I understand that our costs are a challenge for you. If we could put some agency staff in who are trained in the category (not just our products) we can help you improve conversion and get shoppers to trade up".

"Educating the shopper is key. This execution takes away the risk that shoppers sometimes feel when making a purchase".

"I know margin is a key issue right now. Whilst giving you an extra 1% will deliver you an additional $X, growing the category through our initiative to increase conversion, increase the number of items sold and to get people to trade up will deliver $XX. This is equivalent to X% increase in Spend Per Head".

"We are interested in helping the category, not just our brand. By discounting, we are likely to benefit through increased share. Will it drive additional conversion?"

"A free bag is clearly an appeal to some shoppers however, I am sure you will agree that there are hidden costs for you in terms of distributions (damages, space, increased delivery frequency etc). We believe we can cut these costs and bring you simplicity without affecting conversion. With our proposal, we believe we can increase your Spend Per Head and reduce costs...."

"I agree there is an opportunity to cut the price, but will this convert more shoppers and grow absolute sales? Will the growth offset the price discounting?"

"I agree, our performance does appear to show that our sales are in decline. We have checked passenger numbers and they are also down. When we looked at Spend Per Head, it showed that we are actually up year on year. Average price point is down meaning that these discounts have driven conversion or people to buy more. We can help you get a clearer picture. If you could share more detailed sales data on our products, we will come back with a detailed report with key learnings to benefit the category. How does that sound?"

"We believe that a price increase will damage volumes and conversion. This could reduce our SPH by X% and impact the category".

"Our sales growth is in line with passenger growth, but we believe there is an opportunity to perform better and increase Spend Per Head if were given space next to where passengers flow through the store."

"Our sales have been underperforming compared to passenger numbers. We believe that this has been caused by stock issues meaning shoppers are not able to find our products. Let us work with you to manage Minimum Display Quantities and ensure stock levels are correct. This will help reduce lost sales."

"When talking to our store ambassadors, they are highlighting that some [enter nationality] passengers cannot speak [enter language] We would like to bring in [enter language of nationality] speakers to improve conversion".

"Gifting is important in this channel. Our packaging solution helps shoppers see why this product is perfect for gifting or for a self-treat. The aim is to get shoppers to add this to their basket".

"Our sub-category needs to be given more space. It is on-trend right now in other retailers. Giving more space will bring attention to the sub-category and drive incremental sales. This will help increase the overall Spend Per Head".

The key lesson in this section is that you should adapt your language to suit your stakeholders. For example, retailers are not interested in brand terminology. Adapt your approach and it will lead to better relationships and greater success.

GMROII Explained

GMROII stands for Gross Margin Return On Inventory Investment. This calculates the cash margin return on the average stock being held. It is a metric that assesses the ability of the company to convert inventory into cash above and beyond the cost of inventory. This is a metric that is commonly overlooked within Travel Retail but given the size of the stores and the value of some of the product, it should be considered. This is especially so when we consider some of the satellite stores (smaller stores near the gates and away from the main departure lounge area).

The calculation is relatively straightforward:

Gross Profit divided by Average Inventory Cost

Gross profit is calculated by taking revenue and subtracting the cost of goods sold. So, if a retailer has sales of $100m and cost of goods sold is $45m, Gross Profit will be $55m.

Next, we need to understand what the average value of the stock is. This is calculated by using the following formula:

(Current Inventory + Previous inventory) / Number of Periods = Average inventory

This gives you a perspective on how much stock is being held on average. Of course, a retailer's stock holding will fluctuate through the year depending on lead times for deliver, seasonality and rate of sale.

In our example, let us imagine that the average stock holding is $25m. This means that the GMROII can be calculated as:

$$\$55m \ / \ \$25m = 2.2$$

This can be expressed as a ratio or in cash terms. Here we see the ratio is 2.2 or $2.2m of cash generated for every $1m invested in stock. The ratio is above 1 which is positive however some commentators suggest that the aim should be to have a ratio of at least 3.25. I would suggest that in Travel Retail it should be even higher.

So why does this matter in Travel Retail? Well, it is a factor is rarely considered in our channel. New stores are designed with the customer in mind and the space is allocated based on sales. Factoring in GMROII adds an extra dimension.

Imagine for a moment that you have an outer/satellite store. The store sells $500k per year and Gross Profit is $200k. The average stock holding is $200k. The Ratio would be 1 ($200k Gross Profit / $200k average inventory value). Is that the best use of your stock? Sat there gathering dust?

GMROII then is all about driving efficiency within the business. Even if you have a ratio that is far higher than the suggested 3.25, there is always an opportunity to do better.

One factor to consider is space management. If the store is overweight in terms of a high value category, should that space be curbed and given over to a lower value, fast inventory turn category such as Confectionery? It could be argued that if you can reduce space to a category with high stock value and replace it with a category with lower inventory cost and still maintain sales, this will increase efficiency for the retailer.

A Travel Retail Context

To put this into context using a real example (actual numbers have been changed but they are indicative), I will share details of Store A. Store A is a small satellite store situated near the gates. It has been designed to be a 'mini' main store to encourage those who have forgotten to make a purchase in the main departure lounge to come in and shop.

Sales in Store A are $18k a week and the stock holding regularly exceeds $80k. The largest category in terms of stock holding is Beauty with $40k of stock in that store however, sales are under $5k per week for that category. By comparison, Confectionery has $9k of stock with sales of $5k per week.

Purely from a stock turn perspective, Beauty theoretically has a stock turn of 8 weeks if you look at it in terms of value however, when you factor in rate of sale (unit sales), you are looking at 155 days cover.

So, let us assume that Beauty Gross Margin percentage is 60%. On sales of $5k per week, the Gross Margin is going to be $156k for the year ($260k x 60%). With $40k of stock, the GMROII is $3.90 for every $1 of stock held.

Digging into the detail, you discover the at least 50% of the Beauty lines would take 6 months to sell through. Is this the best place for the stock to be sat?

Let us compare Confectionery now. Assuming that the Gross Margin percentage is the same, the sales are the same and therefore the cash margin earned will be the same, a different story emerges. GMROII for Confectionery is $17.44 for ever $1 of stock held in store ($156k / $9k).

Which space and stock is working harder? Beauty or Confectionery?

It is important to remember that space is a limited resource as is stock in the short term. Pockets of stock sat in outer stores or in a warehouse are not in the main store and therefore cannot be sold. So, does it make sense for expensive stock to be there?

In the case of Store A, it was found that by changing the merchandising principles and reducing the range, the stock holding on Beauty could be reduced by a third and increasing Confectionery space would see the following benefits:

- Overall stock held in store is reduced.
- Beauty stock holding is reduced.
- Confectionery stock holding is increased.
- Beauty sales would not be impacted.
- Confectionery sales had potential to increase.
- Replenishment frequency of Confectionery would reduce.
- Beauty stock is freed up to serve other stores.
- Confectionery displays can be more impactful.

All in all, the change in space allocation, range and stock allocation would make the store more efficient and potentially more applicable to the need states of the shopper waiting at the gate. In this particular situation, the retailer chose to stay with the existing execution however, the principles were used in other areas of their business

Key Learning Points

The key learning points in this section are:

- Gross Margin Return On Inventory Investment (GMROII) is a useful metric
- It helps you use stock efficiently and effectively
- It supports space planning to help optimise return on stock investment
- GMROII can lead to other efficiencies such as reducing frequency of replenishment.

Weighted Distribution Explained

Weighted Distribution is an interesting metric that takes a little bit of thought to get your head around, but once you do, it can be most enlightening.

Key account managers for brands can be very focused on increasing their distribution (getting their product into as many stores as possible) however, this is not always the best approach. Let me explain.

Imagine a retailer has 10 stores. You are listed in 5 stores. You might think that 50% coverage is a good position to be in. However, when you look at the sales value for those 5 stores (see the table below), you find that even though you are in 50% of the stores, your brand is only exposed to 23% of the total sales for the retailer. You could be delisted in all of your existing stores and only placed in Store 2 and you would still have the same exposure. Get yourself listed into Store 1 and you will have more than doubled your exposure.

	Sales	Sales Mix	Listed	Sales of listed stores
Store 1	50	39%		
Store 2	30	23%		
Store 3	20	16%	x	20
Store 4	10	8%		
Store 5	5	4%		
Store 6	4	3%		
Store 7	3	2%	x	3
Store 8	2	2%	x	2
Store 9	2	2%	x	2
Store 10	2	2%	x	2
Total	128			29

Percentage of sales the brand is exposed to | 23%

So which should you aim for? Sell out (selling to customers) is a brand's priority however supplying stock to 5 stores is likely to involve more sell-in than to 1 store. This would suggest that a balance needs to be in place. Increasing exposure has its benefits. It means that you can get more stock into the retailer to fill the shelves. The challenge arises when stock isn't selling and either needs to be sold at clearance or returned.

Building a report that enables you to calculate Weighted Distribution will help you:

- identify which stores you should be targeting for your next listing.
- develop a rationale for listing your product in those stores (it is good to go prepared)
- Forecast the potential sales you will gain from listing the products in those locations.
- Build a strong business case to expand your reach.

- Help you budget marketing spend effectively to ensure maximum profitability.

We have been helping our clients build these reports and use them effectively.

Is this a measure you are currently using? If not, what would you do differently now that you know this metric?

Key Learning Points

The key learning points in this section are:

- Weighted Distribution helps you understand WHERE to list
- It uncovers opportunities to increase sales effectively
- Balancing Sell-in vs Sell-out will vary by brand and strategy
- Building these reports can be complex but useful

PART 5

BASKET ANALYSIS

What is Basket Analysis?

Basket analysis is something that I started working on back in 2009 when I was with World Duty Free. The data was particularly difficult to get from their systems at the time but it opened up a whole world of insight that had previously remained hidden.

Since then, I have refined my approach and we have developed software that can do the job.

Basket analysis takes a look into every transaction, takes the findings from each and groups them together to deliver insights. In short, what is it that people often buy together? A simple way to look at this is to consider a lunch purchase. You pop out of the office to a store to pick up a sandwich. Chances are you may also pick up one of the following items:

- A packet of crisps
- A cold drink (coke, fruit juice, water etc)
- A hot drink
- A piece of fruit
- A bar of chocolate
- Some nuts & seeds

- Chewing gum or mints
- A pastry

If the retailer were to dig into the data a little deeper, you might find patterns emerge. It might show that someone who tends to buy a healthy sandwich will go on to buy fruit and water. Those who buy less healthy options might go on to buy "full fat" Coke and a bar of chocolate. When you overlay trend data, you might see a shift emerging. If people are moving away from fatty and unhealthy options of sandwiches towards a more health-conscious options, how should that affect their assortment (their range), how they are merchandised, the quantities on shelf, the communication and point of sale etc. All of this type of data moves retailing from an art to a science. Within Travel Retail, other patterns will emerge too in terms of time of day, destination, nationality etc. All of these things will present opportunities to deepen the understanding of the shopper and help the retailer better serve their customers in the future.

Basket Analysis In Duty Free

You might be surprised to find that up to 50% of transactions can be single item and up to 85% of transactions can be single category (only purchasing Liquor or only purchasing Tobacco etc). When you look at the data from this perspective, it becomes quite a shocking statistic and one that presents a massive opportunity for our channel. What this suggests is that our stores are not designed to encourage cross category purchasing. This is gradually changing with the emergence of single till point locations rather than multiple till sites. This should, however, only be the first step to encouraging greater cross category purchasing.

Question

What would you do differently in store to encourage cross category purchasing?

Having worked in front line retail for many years, I have always believed that it is easier to get someone to buy something else if they already have something in their basket. In the hundreds of hours I have spent watching shoppers in airports, I have seen that this belief holds true. Getting shoppers to pick up a basket, to get one item in that basket and to encourage them to spend more is the key to significant growth within Travel Retail. We must change the way we think about the retail experience and become active sellers of our products.

With this in mind, the easiest category to get into a shopper's basket is Confectionery. Up to 50% of transactions are likely to have Confectionery in them. This is due to the low value, low involvement (doesn't require too much thought or consideration), high impulse nature of the category.

Confectionery encourages shoppers to build their basket (to add more items in) and also is diverse in terms of reasons for purchase (gift, snacking, treat etc). In fact, it is easy for Confectionery shoppers to purchase for multiple reasons (for me, to share, for a gift etc). Unfortunately, Confectionery is often seen as a competitor. It isn't! When you start to evaluate basket data, you see that it is an important category that actually helps the other categories.

So, Basket Analysis is an important (yet underutilised tool). It shows you:

- Which categories are commonly bought together
- Which subcategories are commonly bought together
- Which brands are commonly bought together

Interestingly, basket analysis can also show you which brand or category is likely to drive the behaviour. This insight can have a positive impact on product adjacencies, flow of brands, cross brand promotions etc.

So how would you use Basket Analysis?

- Deeper understanding of shopper behaviour
- Better targeting of destinations and nationalities
- Store design
- Store layouts
- Deciding adjacencies of categories, subcategories and brands
- Better understanding of promotional uptake
- Drives out actions for improving growth
- Developing new assortments
- Testing marketing messages
- Target setting
- Decoding store performances

Basket Analysis and the Shopper

Basket analysis can be relatively time consuming but also rewarding. It is important to try and maximise the value you get from taking time to do the work. Not only will you get amazing insights but you will be able to take this new knowledge forward and find hidden opportunities to grow your business.

Gaining a deeper understanding of the shopper is the obvious big win. If the retailer is capturing flight code and/or nationality, you can evaluate the sales and get even richer insights. This type of analysis can help shape future strategy and shopper research. Right now, a shotgun approach is taken to shopper research and it is ineffective. By using basket data combined with flight codes and nationalities researchers can start targeting their research more effectively. You can ask more of the right questions to the right people in terms of:

- Destination
- Airline
- Nationality
- Purchases
- Brand preferences

Just as you can target people for research purposes, you can also start to target audiences with marketing and merchandising. When I first started using this type of data for destination targeting, the insights were surprising. The in-store team believed that a key target group were buyers of Vodka. When the data was analysed, it turned out that a certain brand of tea was a key purchase.

The store layout was adapted and tea was placed in a prominent position. (Please note, this was quite a controversial decision at the time) but, as predicted, it transformed the performance of the store. The tea was noticed by more of the passenger group that had the propensity to spend which led to increased foot flow and then of course spend.

Remember, all you need to do is get one item in their basket and it opens all sorts of other possibilities.

The key to all basket analysis, though, is that you need to be prepared to experiment. Testing, measuring, evaluating and adjusting are the necessary steps to success. Too much pressure is put on getting things right first time. It is ok to have a theory or a hypothesis and put it to the test. If it doesn't work, as long as you attempt to find out why, that is ok.

Basket Analysis And The Store

By evaluating sales data in a different way, you can begin to see the store design and layout in a very different way. Frequency of purchase adds a different dimension to how you view the sales floor. Some areas that you might think are cold spaces suddenly light up like a Christmas tree. With basket data, you are not reviewing the store in terms of sales value, you are reviewing it in terms of number of shoppers. This gives a better reflection use of space.

The next phase is to consider this in terms of a floor plan. Where are people shopping from? Which aisle? Which fixture? Where do they go from here? What is the path to purchase? (Where is the till?) Is this the right layout? How should the layout be changed to better guide shoppers?

All of the above questions will help an analyst, category teams and store development teams to make decisions on how to improve the space and deliver better results. Of course, this also helps retailers when negotiating space within the store.

The average store is likely to hold thousands of products and the shopper does not have time to consider every single one. What retailers can do however is use past behaviour to observe shopper trends and adapt. Put categories, subcategories and brands together in a way that will seem irresistible to the the shopper. Don't think this can work? Next time you look at Amazon, check out part way down the page of a product you are looking at. It will tell you what people also bought. Their system is busy learning about the things that you like to look at and what other things you might be interested in. Physical stores can do the same although not in real time. Still, it is better than doing nothing.

Basket Analysis and The Future

It is really important that travel retailers consider doing basket analysis on a regular basis. This will help transform performances, deliver a better insight into the shopper and help the businesses make better decisions in terms of ranges, space, merchandising and of course strategy.

We recognise that data is sensitive! That is why we have been developing a piece of desktop software that will enable retailers to evaluate their data without it leaving their business.

Contact me at kevin.brocklebank@oneredkite.com
for more information.

PART 6

SHOPPER MARKETING

Category Management

Developed in the late 80's by Brian Harris, Category Management changed the way suppliers and retailers worked. The process encourages suppliers to work together to focus on the shopper. This enabled retailers to group products together based on the shoppers needs. Each category is then managed as a business unit.

The aim is to serve specific customer groups in the best possible way to maximise every opportunity.

The Category Management Association defines Category management as:

"Trading partners collaborating to decide the point of optimisation in pricing, promotion, shelving and assortment to maximise profitability and shopper satisfaction."

Category Management is based on creating long term partnerships between retailers and suppliers, partnerships ahead of short-term buying decisions. Each party brings their relevant expertise to the table to create ways of best serving the shopper and their needs.

It is essential that the partners are focused on growing the category rather than competing and stealing share.

If sales of category A are £100k and this is made up of Brand Y (£50k) and Brand Z (£50k), the aim should be to focus on growing the category sales to £110k for example. If Brand Y goes on promotion and delivers £60k and Brand Z delivers £40k, the total sales remain at £100k. All that has happened is that sales have been cannibalised. One brand has stolen sales from another.

Category management uses a variety of tools and techniques to grow sales including:

- Promotions
- Assortments (product range)
- Store Layouts
- Space Allocation
- Planograms
- New Product Development
- Activations
- Product enhancements (i.e. think of Chinese New Year sleeves on products)

The easiest way to explain how category management shows up in store is to use examples. Consider Chilled Food. There are a dazzling array of products that come under the heading of Chilled Food however, when you consider WHY the shopper might be buying them, you can begin to group them into segments. These might include:

- Meals for those living alone
- The busy family needing a quick meal at the end of the day
- Lunches that can be heated up in the office microwave
- The Friday Night Takeaway
- Seasonal products (i.e. Christmas)
- The dietary needs (i.e. gluten free, vegan etc)

The category manager may be responsible for each of these segments and will build appropriate ranges, targeted to a specific shopper profile and they will leverage the right space and offers to maximise spend.

Example: The Takeaway Shopper Segment

In supermarkets in the UK, part of their chilled section has been handed over to ready meals. Part of the ready meals section has been given to "takeaways". These takeaways are normally Indian, Chinese, Thai and Italian.

If you choose Indian, there are a selection of main's, side dishes and rice all merchandised together. There will also be naan breads, poppadums, chutneys and other condiments available. Finally, there will usually be beer and wine within easy reach. Sometimes there will be an offer i.e. Dine for £10 where it includes a certain number of mains, sides and a drink.

To grow the category, the retailer will need to do one or more of the following:

- Improve frequency of takeaway nights
- Increase spend through pricing
- Increase spend more items in the basket

The retailer will work with the suppliers to create dishes that will appeal to that shopper segment. This means ensuring that the usual favourites are there but also encourage increased spend. New dishes and regional dishes could also be added to appeal to the more adventurous shoppers.

Bottom line, the retailer and supplier are creating easy solutions to shopper problems. The shopper has one place to go in store, everything is to hand and the assortment is created to ensure that minimum effort is made to make the purchase. There is no fear of forgetting items. It is simple. An offer like the Dine for £10 enables purchases to choose the things they like rather than put up with an item they do not like. This does add complexity however, careful analysis will help guide the retailer and the supplier to ensure the right stock levels and availability.

One point to note is that Dine for £10 does have a shelf life. In time, that may need to move to Dine for £20 as inflation needs to be factored into account.

Example: In The Airport

Category Management will be evident in the airport for Food & Beverage. Companies like Pret a Manger will need to create assortments to appeal to those wanting breakfast, lunch, dinner or snacking. Whilst you can normally get everything all day, the focus of their displays will change throughout the day.

This approach can also be seen in stores such as WH Smiths where different traveller needs are catered for. There are books for the longer journeys, magazines for the shorter journeys, grab and go food, souvenirs, water etc. Almost every need is considered.

For Duty Free retailers, Food & Confectionery might be merchandised by the following categories:

- Onboard (grab and go to eat onboard)
- Healthy Snacks (for the health conscious)
- Sharing (larger items to be consumed over time or shared with others)
- Gifting (premium gifts like boxed chocolates etc)
- Family (brands that appeal to the younger audience)

Once the products have been grouped into their respective categories they can be merchandised on shelf. The example below shows one possible segment flow but this may vary depending on the store location, flow of passengers and other contextual factors.

Onboard	Healthy Snacks	Sharing	Gifting	Family

Example: Decision Trees

Merchandising should take into consideration the shopper decision tree. The easy way to demonstrate a decision tree is to think about buying wine. What steps do you take to buy a wine?

Would you go...

Region ➔ Price ➔ Colour ➔ Grape

Or did you go...

Reason ➔ Colour ➔ Region ➔ Grape ➔ Price

By merchandising products based on decision trees, it can make it easier for the shopper to select what they need and make a purchase. In the example above, Option 2 may have been your preferred route to a decision.

The Category Management Process

1. Define the category

Establishing groups of products in terms of type and shopper need. The example above was the "Takeaway" but in Travel Retail, it might be something else such as "Party Islanders" or "Buckets and Spaders" or "Commuters". Whatever your groups, identify the type of products that these people need and want and organise your range, space, marketing and merchandising around that need.

2. Assess the role of the category

A. Destination

   This is generally a group of products that the retailer is known for. They drive footfall to the store and improves customer loyalty.

B. Core

   These are the products people frequently consume and shoppers seek out regularly. Competition for space and promotions can often be intense. These products are often price sensitive.

C. Convenience

   These are the products that are not routine but are useful for the shopper. These are premium in terms of pricing and enable the shopper to get everything they need in one transaction. Examples might be make-up brushes, travel kits, souvenirs etc.

D. Seasonal

   These are products that appear on a seasonal basis. This might be Chinese New Year, Christmas, Valentines, Mother's Day... It may also incorporate events such as Football, Rugby etc. These products may even become a Destination category at certain times of the year (i.e. Champagne at Christmas). Seasonal products may even create a halo (people who buy the seasonal products also go on to buy other items) effect within other core categories in the store.

3. Assess Performance

A. Complete SWOT analysis (Strengths, Weaknesses, Opportunities & Threats)
B. Evaluate PESTLE factors (Political, Economic, Social, Technological, Legal and Environmental)
C. Sales Data Analysis
  i.   Key sellers (Sales vs Volume)
  ii.   Profit generators
  iii. Basket Analysis
  iv.   Out of stocks / Availability
D. Passenger Numbers (Destination and Nationality if available)
E. Evaluate Spend Per Pax and other metrics

4. Set Objectives and targets

A. Sales
B. Conversion
C. Units Per Basket
D. Spend Per Pax
E. Share
F. Frequency
G. Range size
H. Create dashboards

5. Devise Strategies

A. Traffic Building (Driving Foot flow)
Sometimes referred to as a door busting strategy. Using pricing on price sensitive products to drive footfall into the store. The aim ultimately is to get those shoppers to buy other products whilst they are there. A great example that UK

supermarkets use is Spend over £50 and get 5p off a litre of petrol. When you consider that the average car might hold 50 litres, that will be a saving of £2.50. So, save 5% on your shopping. Not a massive saving but I think that it would encourage people to top up their trolley to make a purchase.

B. Turf Protecting (defending existing sales)

This is where you respond to competition with aggressive promotions and tactics to ensure that your competitors do no steal share. In many ways this is a race to the bottom and a tactic to use sparingly.

C. Transaction Building (i.e. multi packs, multibuys)

Creating offers to encourage people to buy an extra item or items. It might be that bar of chocolate at the till for £1 or it might be getting people to buy multiple items of the same thing (i.e. a triple pack).

D. Profit generating (targeting price increases on high margin and less price sensitive products or own brand).

This is about increasing prices on secondary items rather than destination items or known value items (items that the customer knows how much a product is when asked). It might be that a retailer knows that the shoppers main purchase is a TV (which needs to be competitive) but put the price up on batteries. Yes, the shopper could probably buy cheaper elsewhere but it is the convenience that makes purchasing there and then attractive.

E. Excitement Generating Strategy

Usually a lifestyle orientated position for products. This is something that engages the shopper and that is beyond the normal everyday experience. It is likely to be seasonal products that create the biggest wow factor. An example of excitement generating executions might be the Raffles Bar that was in Singapore airport at DFS. Unfortunately, it was on the upper floor so was probably missed by a lot of shoppers. Nice idea, a better execution might have been to place it out in front of the store on the concourse.

F. Cash Generation (focus on high volume / frequent purchase)
This will be a category like Confectionery within Travel Retail. Fast moving, good margin, impulse purchase, low stock value. This category enables the retailer to generate cash rather than have it sat on shelves. Check out the Gross Margin Return On Inventory Investment piece in the Metrics section of this book.

G. Image Enhancing Strategy (drive image and loyalty through quality, service, presentation etc.)
Well, Travel Retail is full of brands and products that enhance the image of the airport shopping experience. Super premium stores, connoisseur zones and high end brands all add to the image of the airport.

6. Set Category Tactics

A. Product (including availability)
Make sure you have the right products in the right quantities to serve the shopper. Make sure you gather intelligence from the front line. Is there anything that the shoppers are asking for? Is there a pattern to these requests? Are people seeking out a new niche subcategory? Also, make sure that the stock quantities are correct to make replenishment as efficient as possible and reduce out of stocks.

B. Price
Are the products you have hitting the right need? Is the range too premium or too cheap for the shopper profile of that location?

C. Place

Have you got the right products in the right place? Undertake a gap analysis to identify where there are opportunities to list products in the store portfolio. Ensure that distribution is efficient and effective.

D. Promotion

Do you need to promote? If so, do you have the right promotional mechanic in the right locations? For example, a European wide promotion with one mechanic on a specific brand is unlikely to work in Travel Retail. Make sure that the promotions you run are delivering a return on investment.

E. People

Do you have the right people in place? Do they buy into your vision and support it? Or are they there for a pay cheque? Find the right people who have a passion for retail and giving customers a great experience.

F. Process

Are all of your processes as efficient as they can be? Is there room for improvement? What are the opportunities to step change what you do? Certainly if you do not have a space planning function, this is one opportunity to improve cross functional working and improve efficiencies.

G. Physical Evidence

Are all of the fixtures in a good state of repair, clean and fit for purpose? Is the signage clear and easy to understand? Are staff well groomed in a standard uniform? Is the till point free from debris? Are the aisles clear and easy for shoppers to navigate with a travel bag? Physical Evidence relates to all the tangible elements of the store that people see and interact with?

7. Implement

A. Have A Plan

Once the above has been completed, it is imperative that a clear plan is created with clear milestones. This planning process needs to ensure that all stakeholders are aligned and/or informed. Clear deadlines need to be given to ensure that everything is delivered on time to ensure that dependencies (the subsequent tasks) are not affected.

B. Give Feedback Quickly

No plan survives first contact and there will be variables that require a plan to change. The key is to be quick and unemotional about giving feedback. This enables the business to be responsive and adapt to change quickly and effectively. Enabling others to have autonomy to make decisions will ensure that the plans can be adapted with minimum lead times.

C. Ensure Accountability

It is essential that each stakeholder takes ownership and responsibility their stage(s) of the plan. This makes them accountable for the success and failures of each project. This prevents individuals side-stepping deadlines and commitments.

8. Review

A. Avoid Avoidance

Often, there is a lot of focus on creating business cases for new projects but very little follow up and evaluation after the event. The 2 key reasons for this is either 1) the commercial team moves on to new shiny projects, or, 2) there is a fear that the exercise was not the success it was planned to be so the reaction can sometimes be "let's not shine a light on it".

B. Learn & Adapt

Always do a review, whatever you think the outcome might be. It is essential to learn from what has happened in the past. Whilst the past performances do not always act as a perfect indicator for future performances, it does provide some guidance.

The Category Manager

This role focuses on combining insights from sales data, research from a wide variety of sources and manufacturer knowledge to help make better decisions and strategies. The ambition is to continually drive growth and profitability in a way that leads to customer satisfaction.

The category manager will:

- Undertake regular range reviews
- Monitor rates of sale
- Check on availability
- Monitor customer loyalty
- Evaluate promotional effectiveness
- Review visual merchandising to consider
  o Navigation
  o Segmentation
  o Flow
  o Brand blocking (grouping brands together) vs Segment blocking (grouping similar types of products together)
  o Multi-siting (putting products in strategic places to maximise effectiveness
  o Space evaluation and optimisation

Travel Retail have the opportunity to embrace category management to ensure that they maximise shopper spend.

Category management can bring a range of benefits including:

- Improved sales and profitability
- Increased customer satisfaction
- Better availability
- Fewer out of stock items
- Less wastage
- Reduced costs

Meet AIDA

Back at college, one of the first lessons I had in Marketing was that there are 4 key components when it comes to advertising. No, I am not talking about the 4 P's just now. I am talking about the AIDA model, developed in 1898 by an American businessman called Elias St Elmo Lewis. AIDA stands for:

Attract Attention

This is all about eyeballs.... getting people to see your brand in the crowd, to stand out. In today's crowded world, it is difficult to cut through the noise of marketing messages that people see all day, every day. With social media, there are marketing messages everywhere. Ever been on Instagram or Facebook and found yourself mindlessly scrolling? Put into today's digital world, is what you are showing the customer enough to stop them scrolling on their phone or tablet?

Maintain **I**nterest

This is about holding the person's attention, to connect with them in a way that generates a level of curiosity or interest. If they are thinking about your brand, your product or your service in a way that requires extra thought, you have their interest. The question here is are you being considered in a positive light? What is the hook? If they have stopped scrolling, why should they hang around? With an in-store activation, very often it will be in an unmissable position (you have their attention) but will they engage? Will they walk over and interact? Will they ask questions?

Create **D**esire

Creating desire has a clue, a big one. Desire is an emotional response. It may be interpreted as a want or a need. Ever seen something and you just 'had' to have it? A computer? A watch? A pair of shoes? Or a dress maybe? Whatever it is, it seems to take up residence in your head and you start to assess whether to buy it or not. This is where active selling becomes incredibly effective. If you have strong will power, you may just walk away. A sale is lost. Active selling can actually be enough to tip a shopper into the final stage.

Take **A**ction

This is the goal of any business - to get potential buyers to take action. That action might be to sample the product or to buy the product right there. Shoppers acting and buying is what keeps the doors open and the shop trading. This is the critical final step.

When you think about it, the AIDA model is like a funnel really.

1. You are not going to capture everyone's attention (whatever you might think!).
2. Those whose attention you do get, may not be interested.
3. Those who are interested, may find that what you offer isn't what they want.
4. Those who really desire your product may not be able to buy that product right now.

This is often a numbers game.

Let's walk through an example that relates to Travel Retail. AIDA, can be applied to other aspects of marketing where you need engage with people. In Travel Retail, Activations are a clear example of this.

Whisky Brand X has decided to take a promotional slot in Airport Y. Taking a realistic view, not everyone will see it and not everyone will be interested (a shock to some of you but not everyone likes or has a need for Whisky).

Let's assume for every 100 people that come through the airport, the Activation catches the attention of 70 people and of those 70 people, 20 are curious enough or interested enough to wander over to your activation.

The chances are that 10 of them will "taste and waste". This means that they will try the liquid and walk away. You know the type - they are on holiday and they are heading to the airport bar and will pick up the free samples on the way through.

Another 7 will give your brand and product fair consideration and are in the balance. We will call them the "Undecided". These are the ones that need to be "sold" to. The sparks of interest need to be fanned into flames and a sense of need or wanting must be uncovered.

Finally, the last 3 will be interested enough and engaged enough to buy your product. They are likely to be familiar with your brand or certainly have an awareness of it. They may even have bought in store even if no-one was there to offer a sample and tell them the story behind the brand.

So, it is the other 7, the "undecided" that are there to be influenced. To do this, the activation needs to be well executed, connect and engage with the shopper but also needs the right people to bring it to life. Time and time again, we have seen staff on activations who lack product knowledge, brand knowledge and the skills to actually sell. Anyone can stand there with a silver tray and dish out samples. It makes it easy for those "taste and waste" sample hoovers to come along and take your stock.

People then, are the thing that can make the biggest difference. Yes, you can have information show cards, digital screens and other ways of communicating your brand story but it is people that can connect on an emotional level.

Retail is all about selling product. Going back to the days before supermarkets, retailers had small stores with products on shelves behind a counter and people were served by the shop owner. This led to a small but curated range that appealed to the local market. The vendor would have a good knowledge of the products they sold and gave suitable advice to the shopper.

With the introduction of the supermarket, ranges expanded seemingly exponentially. Filling the space was as important as trying to appeal to customers to spend more.

Now, a new breed of supermarkets have emerged in the form of low cost retailers such as Aldi and Lidl. Smaller stores, a concise range and rapid service (if you have ever been to one of these stores you will know what I mean!). Shoppers save money thanks to costs being stripped out, leaving a bare bones shopping experience.

Over the years, the retail offer in airports have expanded significantly. Larger stores in big airports with these same key core categories. More brands have been introduced (particularly in Beauty) to appeal to a wider audience. More brands means more products. More products means more choice and more choice... Well... that can lead to confusion and, worse still, a loss in sales.

In 2000, an experiment was undertaken by psychologists (Lyngar & Lepper) to understand the effect of range size on purchase decisions. They offered a wide variety of jams and found that despite much interest, they only sold a few. When the experiment was run again, they offered only 3 different jams. Sales increased significantly. The phrase Fewer, Bigger, Better springs to mind.

Offer fewer products, make a bigger statement of them and present them in a better way to do achieve better sales.

When it comes to building an assortment or completing a range review, there are a number of questions that need to be answered:

- Who is shopping?
- What are they buying?
- Why are they buying?
- How are trends changing things?
- How to Evaluate the assortment
- The 80/20 Rule
- Nationality vs Destination
- Does Pricing play a role?
- Is there a show piece that can be used?

The main question I always come back to is why shoppers buy? It is often overlooked by retailers and brands. Brands will often talk about the need to increase distribution or they might focus on the features and benefits but not the rationale / reason why retailers have it. There is little focus on the rationale for the purchase. Why would a customer buy this particular product?

When brands are looking to get new products listed, it is important to present a valid reason for listing it in the retailers stores. They (the retailer and the customer) do not want any more "me too" products. "Me too" products are products that have no real discernible difference to competitor products. If a retailer has 3 different 300g bars of chocolate with almonds in, do they really need a 4th?

Creating Categories

One option is to consider creating your own distinct subcategory. If you have identified a unique use or customer segment for your product, use it to best effect by becoming a category leader in your own category.

For example, you may have developed an alcohol-free spirit that would appeal to those who do not want to drink or cannot drink alcohol for religious reasons. Propose a new subcategory to the retailer which will require space to represent it properly. It may mean that a whole bay is required, a communication plan, staffing to do samples etc. Admittedly it would require competitor brands to be introduced to enable a credible range but if your brand can act as the signpost, all the better. You are taking the first move advantage.

Of course, there are no duties on alcohol free products however, there may just be a market opportunity. Remember, it is about trying to appeal to a new customer base and get them spending.

Another example might be vegan chocolate. Should that be in the same section hidden amongst regular chocolate? Or should there be a dedicated space that appeals to a niche shopper. Vegan can also double up as a "Free From Dairy" space.

Apply Pressure On Your Competition

However you use the AIDA model or the whether you seek to create a new subcategory, the aim should be to apply pressure on your competition by create new perspectives for the shopper. In todays world where it is becoming increasingly difficult to get attention and hold it, resonating with the shopper is ever more important.

People Filter Out Messages

People are bombarded with thousands of messages every single day. To cope with the volume of messages we filter out what is not relevant. Public Relations companies will talk about "Opportunities to See" when they get press releases into a paper however relevance plays a MASSIVE role. For example, imagine you are a cosmetics brand and have got an article in a travel magazine about a new moisturiser. The magazine has a circulation of 100,000. The article is in the Beauty Section of the magazine. Because of the nature of the product (for women) it will probably be filtered out by men. Not all women will see that page and when they do, not everyone will read it. Finally, you are at a place where it might lead to a handful of sales.

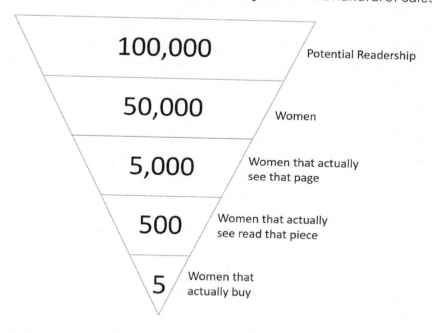

To improve the performance, one option is to grow the readership. To double sales, you would need to go from 100,000 to 200,000 based on those ratio's which is no easy feat. The easier option is to increase relevance, appeal and interest by communicating with your target customer in a way that is compelling. Imagine that the moisturiser is vegan. By creating an article that appeals to vegans, still fairly niche at the time of writing, it is likely to stand out and attract vegan readers.

Strategy, Targeting & Positioning

To develop an effective strategy, you need to understand what has been driving sales and how trends have changed. Rather than focusing on product, the STP approach is about focusing on the commercially important audiences and creating relevant and relatable messages to appeal to them.

The process is as follows:

Segmentation	The market (for example, an airport) should be segmented into key customer groups. The easiest option is to segment by destination as this data is normally captured at the point of purchase. Nationality is an option if that data is captured however, this is very a very broad scope.
Targeting	Once you have your segments in place, you can evaluate past performances to identify the size of the market and the potential opportunities available. Select one or more segments that you wish to target.
Positioning	Once you have segments that you want to target, it is about creating a proposition that will appeal to that specific audience. It is about leveraging the marketing mix to 'speak' to those you are trying to target.
Plan & Deploy	Once you have a plan, you must deploy your resources in the right way to maximise your return on investment.

Segmentation

There are a variety of ways to segment your audience depending on the availability of information. These include:

- Demographics (age, gender, income, education, ethnicity, marital status etc)
- Psychographics (attitudes, lifestyle, hobbies, personality traits)
- Lifestyle (hobbies, interests)
- Beliefs & Values (Religious, political, cultural)
- Life stage (based on chronological age -18 – 30's holidays vs Saga (over 50's) holidays)

Some of the airlines and travel companies are excellent at understanding WHY passengers are travelling and giving them what they want. For example, Jet2 are very good at segmenting their holidays to appeal to different audiences (correct at the time of writing):

- Vibe holidays for the younger audience who want to party
- Indulgent Escapes for the affluent audience who want luxury and simplicity
- City Escapes for those looking for a cultural experience

There are of course other categories but these offer a good demonstration of how one travel company targets the different reasons and motivations for travel. Does a family who want to enjoy an 'Indulgent Escape' want to end up in a party hotel with noisy occupants that are hungover around the pool the next day? No! Segmenting holidays in this way gives travellers confidence that they will not end up in the wrong place.

An example of segmenting holidays might look like this (this is an example only):

| | Holiday | | | | Trip | |
	Beach	Explore	Active	Cruise	Short Break	Business
Solo	-	X	X	O	X	O
Couples	O	O	O	O	O	-
Friends	O	-	X	-	O	-
Family - Young	X	-	O	O	-	-
Family - Teen	X	X	X	O	X	-
Family Gathering	O	-	-	-	O	O

x	Most Likely
o	Possibly
-	Least Likely

In Travel Retail, there are other ways of creating segments and these can include:

- Nationality
- Destination (where are they travelling to?)
- Reason for travel (business, leisure, city break, visiting family & friends etc)
- Carrier (low cost carrier vs full service carrier)
- Seat selection (First Class, Business, Premium Economy & Economy)
- Frequency (Loyalty card holders, Lounge users)

However you split your customer base, the segment(s) need to be economically viable. Therefore, if you are to invest in a marketing program, the outcome needs to pay for itself and deliver incremental value.

I am sure there are many other ways of segmenting using a wide array of variables depending on the amount of information available.

For retailers that have more than one airport, there are opportunities to learn from whole business. If you are particularly successful at selling specifically to people flying to Norway in Airport A but that destination underperforms in Airport B, what is driving that?

Example

To establish which destinations you want to target, you might use a positioning map like this:

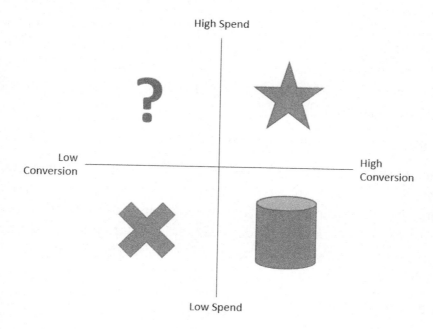

Star – High Spenders / High Conversion

Destinations that fall into this section are a key target for a retailer. They have a propensity to shop and spend. The flights heading to this destination should be a key focus and should ensure that the brands and products that have the broadest appeal are in key line of sight locations.

Question Mark – High Spenders / Low Conversion

The passengers that fall into this quadrant are High Spenders but only a few convert to shoppers. Further investigation would be required to understand what they buy, which airline they travel on and at what time of day they are likely to fly. The key is to find out what unlocks better conversion.

Barrel – High Conversion / Low Spend

This audience is likely to be the 'bread and butter' in terms of sales. This section will be about volume of transactions. Destinations with higher conversion but a lower than average spend will require a different strategy. This might be about aiming to get one extra item into their basket, or maybe more attention could be paid to whether their main purchase through impulse. Different tactics can be deployed to deliver that.

Cross - Low Conversion / Low Spend

This audience is the most challenging to convert and drive value from. There may be a number of reasons why this destination is not spending much, ranging from allowances, currency exchange rates or a lack of appropriate brands. Whilst it is tempting to target this group, there may be more commercially important destinations available that would generate a better return on marketing spend.

One Caveat – Number of Passengers

While it can be tempting to just view Destinations in terms of Conversion and Spend, it is also important to factor in passenger numbers. If you have a Star destination but only a small number of passengers flying to that location, it will be incredibly difficult to generate significant incremental sales. It is important to overlay passenger numbers to be able to quantify the 'size of prize'.

Applied Example – Destination 'Alpha'

Once you have established how each of your Destinations spend and convert you find out that destination 'Alpha' are in the "Question Mark" square. Further investigation shows that there are a good number of passengers that travel to that Destination and that if you converted more passengers, even at a lower spend, it would deliver significant incremental sales. Digging into the sales data, you find that buyers who fly to "Alpha" tend to shop premium Cognacs and Whiskies. There are particular flights that see significant sales and you discover that you have speakers for that nationality in store at that time. It would be reasonable to assume that there is a language barrier preventing people from converting from shoppers to buyers.

You run some further analysis and discover that there are another 20 flights that go to Alpha but you do not have anyone who can speak the language in store during that time. You select 3 key flights and put 2 people who can speak their language in store during those times as a test. You see enough incremental sales to cover the cost of the additional staffing from that Destination. You also have the halo benefit from the additional head count in store serving passengers.

Next, you consider adding signage in that language near the brands that they prefer. Once again, you test this and that too leads to further incremental gains. From here, there are a number of other options available to effectively target that destination including:

- Adapting merchandising displays to target that audience at key times
- Using targeted offers for those flights to drive revenue
- Tap into the calendar and cultural opportunities
- Experiment with the assortment to encourage further trade up

- Utilise basket data to identify the products most likely bought with their main item
- Create a highly targeted research project to better understand those travelling to that destination
- Create a workshop / focus group with those staff that serve the destination to better understand what those passengers are looking for and how you can best serve those needs.

Once this has been completed, larger retailers can transfer their learnings into other airports and test the effectiveness.

The key is to not get too focused on an individual Destination or nationality. In Travel Retail in the UK it used to be all about those flying to America, then flying to Japan, then Russia and towards the end of my time there it was all about those flying to Nigeria. Of course, as time has gone on, it is now about China. The danger of zeroing in on one Destination or Nationality is missed opportunities and lost sales.

Product

Within Retail, Product is a key element of the marketing mix. It is about having the right range (also known as an assortment) to appeal to the broadest customer base. Creating the right mix of Categories, Subcategories, Brands and Products will ensure that customers have an appropriate choice.

Using an example outside of Travel Retail – Bicycles. There are a vast range of Bicycles available from balance bikes for children through to high end carbon fibre bikes that professionals and serious enthusiasts will ride. A bike shop will need to establish their key target audience and their customers needs to select an appropriate range. If you are targeting the enthusiast, your range / assortment will be focused on the higher end of the customer spectrum. If you are targeting families, you are likely to have a product range geared towards children's bikes and family appropriate bikes.

As physical stores do not have rubber walls, it is important to decide which products to purchase. There is also the issue of stock management, merchandising displays and ensuring that the offer is displayed in the most appropriate way.

Over the last decade or so, Travel Retail has pushed for "Exclusives" or products that cannot be sourced in shops. This might be in the form of different sizes, different packaging or a completely different format. Exclusives have been used in Domestic retail to good effect. For example, years ago, manufacturers of white goods would sometimes make a small adjustment to a product so that they could sell essentially the same product under different model numbers to different retailers. This means that the product was "differentiated" and therefore avoid direct price competition. By having products in different sizes, it becomes difficult to do a direct comparison on price.

With the focus on health, pack sizes of chocolate have gradually become smaller and smaller but it could be argued that prices have remained constant. This drives additional profitability without "increasing" prices.

Other ways of differentiating a product is to tie it to the locality or to a calendar event. This can be done through packaging. It may be a special sleeve that covers the product to turn it into a souvenir gift or it may be something that celebrates a date like Chinese New Year. Whatever the occasion, event or location, adapting an existing product through packaging can give shoppers more reason to purchase. This is likely to be extended into sports, music, festivals and other events that drive people to travel through airports.

It is important that a credible range is built to factor in the following principles and product types:

- **Signpost Brands**

  These are the brands that help the shopper locate the category. Within Travel Retail, these are likely to be global brands but could as easily be local brands, depending on the strength of that brand. An example might be Bombay Sapphire for Gin.

- **Good, Better, Best**

  Which lines do you need to create a Good (entry level), Better (mid-price point), Best (high end / premium). This helps the shopper trade up a price ladder. This can be created by using features and / or pack size to help the shopper.

- **Theatre Lines**

  These may be lines which you may rarely sell but act as a show piece. I once heard a story about a fishmonger who had a sharks head in his fish display cabinet. Although he didn't expect to sell the sharks head, the display was a talking point in the store and spread positive word of mouth.

- **Niche Brands / Lines**

  Once you have your main key brands, which niche brands should be stocked to attract another audience. These are the lines that the aficionado's will seek out. An example might be someone who has developed a specific taste for a niche chocolate. The brand will not be a mainstream brand and it will have a distinct customer following.

- **WIGIG lines (When it's gone, it's gone)**

  These are lines that are bought in, probably on a special deal and when they have sold through they will not be replaced. These products play a specific role within the category and this could be anything from Traffic Driving (i.e. special discounted deal) through to Basket Building (i.e. a Christmas soft toy).

- **Bolt-on lines**

  These are lines where the brand insists that if you want to stock line X, you will need to also range Y, Z, A in the same stores. These lines need to be accounted for in some way and add to the space requirements.

- **Impulse Lines**

  These are the types of products that take little thought and people buy on impulse. It may be a chocolate bar, it may be a lip balm or even a soft toy. It is something that makes the shopper think – oh go on then!

However you approach the task of ranging, it is important to think about the shopper and what it is that THEY are likely to buy.

Pricing

Pricing in Travel Retail is one of those perennial battles and hot topics of discussion. The challenge that retailers have is that concession fees are high and that growth historically has come from increasing passenger numbers and price rises (or premiumisation of products). As more expensive products are made available, it appeals to fewer shoppers. Despite this, total sales have managed to grow. The retailers are therefore achieving greater sales off of less shoppers.

In addition to this, the price of existing products have risen or 'exclusives' have been listed. It is not easy for the shopper to do a price comparison. Exclusives are often more expensive gram for gram and this impacts perceived value. The problem now is that the price points are getting to a level where it is no longer competitive with other channels. The value proposition of Travel Retail has been eroded.

At the time of writing, Dixons Travel Retail had just closed at the airports. This is unsurprising as the EU / NEU Duty and Tax-Free rules had changed in the UK. When you go to the airport, you expect

Tax Free or Duty-Free products. The problem with Dixons was that the price was pretty much the same as what you could pay in a local store. There was no financial benefit to shopping at the airport. It was merely convenience. I only ever shopped at Dixons when I absolutely needed to (usually when I had forgotten something). The UK government could see that savings were not being passed on and so it would appear that the inevitable happened, the legislation changed. What I am saying is – when there is no longer a price differentiation between "Tax Free" and "Tax Paid" something needs to give.

One common theme that you will pick up on in this book is that each airport is different as each airport has a different passenger profile even though there are usually clusters that can be found across a region where "similar" airports show similar spend profiles.

Now that retailers footprints are expanding through mergers and consolidation, pricing needs to have careful attention. Price perception is therefore influenced over the range / assortment and what you have showing up as your lead product. So – if you the price ceiling for a particular product category is €39, it makes little sense to be promoting and emphasising products at €59. Shoppers in that particular location are likely to perceive it to be an expensive store even though the €39 products are readily available for purchase (but hidden).

Price Competitive

Retailers try to overcome price competitiveness through differentiation and "Travel Retail Exclusives". This means that there is not a comparative product to enable price benchmarking or price checking. The only place it can be bought is at the airport. This differentiation is usually a different pack size or different design in terms of packaging but I can see a time where these minor differences will no longer be enough to hold water.

High Street vs International

Where should price comparisons be taken? Should it be versus the stores local to the airport or should it be compared to other airports across an international cluster? This is a tricky question because it should depend on the profile / mix of the shoppers. You also have the complex problem of currency fluctuations that will influence prices and make some points of purchase super competitive. Of course, the other option is online pricing. The likes of Amazon are becoming increasingly THE go to place to buy virtually anything and brands are rapidly getting to grips with Direct To Consumer.

The problem with price comparison across other retailers is the frustration it is likely to cause the shopper. To explain this, I will use The Cup Of Tea Dilemma!

You are flying from A to B. When you travel you usually use "SuperCheap Airline" but on this occasion, you need to fly with "Notquitesocheap". You sit down in your seat, the plane takes off and the trolley comes around. You know that a coffee on "SuperCheap" is €2.50. The coffee on "Notquitesocheap" is priced at €3.50. You are pretty sure it is the same brand of coffee. You are thirsty. What do you do?

Chances are you will probably have a grumble and pay the price. You will purchase the coffee and have done with it. You recognise that you will need to pay more but it isn't the end of the world. You might not have that biscuit though!

So, here we have a situation where the pricing for essentially the same product is significantly different. It is a low involvement purchase meaning that little thought or mental engagement needs to go into making the purchase decision. You have a choice – you buy or you don't. The need is great so you make the purchase.

The interesting question would be, how far could the price be pushed before you decided to skip the coffee... €4? €4.75? €5? We all have a zone of tolerance depending on how much we are in need of a particular product.

Now, let's take a look at Travel Retail products. You want to buy a product in Duty Free. You go to pick it up and you see the product is $50. You realise that the product in the shops at home is $60 (great, there is a saving) but you can buy it online for $47. What do you do? Well? If you need it now, you will probably buy it. Are you willing to wait and order it online to save $3? Probably not.

You remember a friend telling you that there is a price comparison site online that tells you the prices of products at different airports around the world. You go online and search this particular product. You find it for $38 at another airport. That is a $12 saving. The problem is, you are not in that airport! Take a moment to consider how this makes you feel about your purchase. Suddenly it is starting to feel like you are paying over the odds for the product in that location. Do you still buy it?

Part of you will want to go ahead with the purchase because you want the product right now. Part of you will feel uncertain because you do not want to be ripped off. If you do go ahead with the purchase, you will feel like that the retailer is not giving value.

The problem with sites like this is the lack of context. It does not give you information on the price of products in the local market for comparison. The product may still be cheaper at the airport compared to the stores in the local area. The other factor to consider is that the store that has the price of $38 might have some terms and conditions relating to that price.

Finally, there is no consideration to the location. What if that product is $38 because it is down the road from the place it is made and the airport you are considering buying it from is in New York? What about the currency exchange rates, the transportation costs, administration costs, storage costs etc?

Price comparisons across airports and countries lead to very dangerous ground for our industry. Are price comparison sites inevitable? Probably. It is one more thing that is trying to put a hammer into the coffin of Travel Retail. Shoppers will need to be persuaded, educated and influenced at the point of purchase. This means less reliance on people selling themselves the product or using phones to make their decisions. It involves active selling and cross selling to maximise every shopper opportunity.

Low-Cost Airlines vs Full-Service Carriers

Pricing is interesting when it comes to flights. Low-cost airlines have deconstructed their offer so that you only pay for what you need. The thing is, by the time you have added everything back in, is it any cheaper? In some respects, it is even more expensive and you pay for the privilege of dashing to the gate and getting into a queue. How come those priority boarding queues are so long?

What people are drawn into is the prospect of a cheaper flight. The purchaser feels like they are in control of what they are paying for.

The thing is, you often see different passenger profiles boarding the low-cost airline vs the full-service airline. On the low-cost airlines you tend to see younger passenger, hardened air warriors and those who are happy to forego some of the comforts and privileges that full-service carriers offer. This is also reflected in the spend behaviours that you see in the transaction data. Spends tend to be lower for low-cost carrier passengers compared to full-service and as such, airports tend to put those flights at gates that are at the furthest end of the airport. Those that are more likely to spend are going to put at gates near the shops so they have more dwell time to spend.

Are low-cost carrier passengers more price sensitive compared to full-service passengers? It is worth further investigation.

Price Ladder

If you have never heard of the term "Price Ladder" it is a relatively simple concept to understand. If we consider a product category – let's use Gin as the example. If your entry level price point is £18 and the highest priced product that you have available is £60 – there is a big gap. If you only had those two products available, the higher price item seems like a massive jump up. The higher priced product seems incredibly difficult to justify. This is why we need to add more products in-between to make it easier to "trade up".

The shopper might not necessarily want the entry level price point for a whole variety of reasons. There is a perception that cheap means poor quality and so people often try to by the second cheapest. This is a common occurrence in the food service industry. Add in another product at say £24 (yes, it is closer to £20 than it is to £30) and you have the perception that it is reasonably priced but not the cheapest. Still, the gap between £24 and £60 is still big. We need to add more rungs onto the ladder.

A retailer will review the range of brands and bottle sizes to come up with a range of products that enables the shopper to select a product which best suits their budget. Want something to go into a punch – entry level is probably going to be a preferred choice. Want something that will be a nice gift for someone – mid to high price point might be the product that best suits them.

With products like electricals, it can be a little easier to create a price ladder as there are many features, advantages and benefits that you can use to add more to the price.

Retailers can often use a high price point to trick the shopper into thinking something is more reasonably priced. So, put the £24 product next to the £60 and suddenly £24 looks cheap. In fact, you could probably put a £35 product or a £40 product next to the £60 one and they too look more reasonably priced. By placing the £60 product into the range, it recalibrates people's perception of what they think is reasonable for a price point.

Of course, you will find some people who will naturally gravitate to the most expensive products you have and that is all they will buy. Also, you will have those who will want to buy the cheapest possible product or go for the lower end of the pricing ladder. The one common theme that I have observed is that the sales data often backs this up. You end up with a wasteland in the middle of the price ladder where there are either few products and/or few sales. This polarity in sales is something that needs to be addressed and presents a real opportunity for retailers. A lot of emphasis is placed on self-serve however, if people are left to their own devices and decision making, they are likely to move to one end of the spectrum or another. This means that you are likely to have shoppers trade down and this is lost revenue.

So, how can this dip in the middle be fixed?

One approach is to leverage salespeople who can actively encourage people to trade up and buy more expensive products. Even when sales people are deployed, they can often go for the easy sale and not proactively encourage people to spend more but going above their perceived budget. The salesperson can encourage shoppers to take steps up the pricing ladder by helping the shopper make better and more informed decisions.

Another approach is to work on the merchandising standards to encourage trade up. This might involve using price logic (highest price at the top of the fixture, lowest price at the bottom).

One option could be to work on activations that give focus to key lines within the middle price point of the category.

Finally, the shopper needs a reason to buy or to trade up to the next price point. Information will normally help with this. In the absence of salespeople, information in the form of ticketing, point of sale or digital displays will help them make their decision. Promotions combined with merchandising will help the buyer make a jump from one product to another unless they are brand loyal. Even then, they can sometimes be nudged.

Some careful analysis of what price points work best for which brands and that will help you uncover the right pricing strategy. It will help you establish the right price ladder for a specific location. Remember, every airport is different and what works in one location might not work in another.

I once heard a story about a fishmonger who used to buy sharks head's for their display. Of course, no-one would want to buy the sharks head but it was a reason to come into the shop. It was different, it was fascinating and once there, people made the decision to buy some fish. Was the shark's head really necessary? Well, in theory no. BUT it was a point of difference from any other fishmonger or butcher. It was interesting. Retailers will often try to find something that will draw people into the store or category to make a purchase. Crème de la Mer used to have fish tanks in stores. Not something you would expect to see in an airport and that was precisely the point. It was different, it attracted attention and was of course, completely on brand for them given the nature of their product.

Price Elasticity

I have touched on a point above about running analysis on prices. This is something that I would highly recommend to better understand the effect of changes in prices. This relates to price elasticity – or the effect of a change in price based on demand for the product. There are some things that are price inelastic. Take petrol for example, the price of petrol can fluctuate quite significantly (it does recently in the UK) but because we are creatures of routine, we are unlikely to make drastic changes to our travel plans and so we tend to just spend regardless of changes in prices.

In the chart below, we see a relatively low reduction in demand despite a significant increase in price. This is an example of where something is price inelastic.

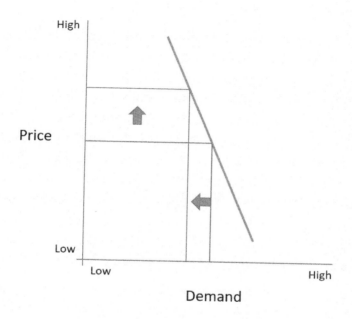

Other products might be highly price sensitive and therefore a change in price is likely to trigger a significant change in demand or a switch to a competitors product.

One product category that is well known for this is Dishwasher Tablets. Shoppers will go for the product that is on offer – there is little brand loyalty. There will be other products and categories that you buy where if the price changes even a small amount it might affect your purchasing behaviour.

In the past I have run a number of analysis projects to identify the tipping point on prices. There was a Perfume project I ran across a region that took in over 2 years of sales history and it monitored the changes in prices of key lines to establish how far the client could shift prices and not impact demand. The overall ambition was to be able to create region wide standard promotional mechanic. The subsequent results showed that this was going to be commercially unviable. This is due to every location being different. We were able to identify clusters of similar behaviour which meant a different promotional strategy needed to be developed.

The key findings showed that in some locations the highest tolerated price point for a fragrance stood at €39 in some locations, whilst in others, the highest price points stood at €57. So what did this tell the brand client? It told them that some lines could tolerate a small price increase as long as it stayed under the €40 price point. It told them that different brands should be focused in on in other locations. These brands could have products discounted (promotional activity) from €65 down to €57 and it would trigger an uplift in demand that would be great enough to offset the lost sales through the discount. The next question we left them with is would higher demand be sustained if the new price remained at the lower price of €57. This was never tested and so I cannot comment on this.

Pricing is something that is rarely assessed in great detail both in retailers and in brands, however it does present a unique opportunity to drive additional demand. Triggering a shopper to buy through pricing is one thing that Travel Retail needs to focus on. There are so many different variables to consider when pricing including the following:

- Local market prices
- Key benchmarking airport prices
- Currency fluctuations
- Profit margins and costs
- Supplier support and funding
- Key competitor pricing strategies
- Supply & availability

One interesting concept with pricing is the level of supply. A clever and interesting strategy was deployed for Cloudy Bay wine. When it was launched, it wasn't easy to get hold of or so customers were led to believe. At the time, it was being sold at a premium compared to what the average consumer was paying for wine. Despite this, everyone seemed to know someone who had "one last case out the back". The scarcity led people to believe that it was in high demand and popular so people would go out of their way to get it. Scarcity facilitates a price premium.

Another example of how exclusivity and scarcity work is the new social media platform, Clubhouse. It was invitation only access and when people joined they got 2 invites that they could use to share with others. This made the invites rare and not unlike a form of currency. There was value to those invites and if someone you knew invited you to join, it was almost a sense of validation that you were worthy to be on that platform. Interestingly, when I finally went to get onto the platform, I joined a waiting list but was 'in' within a few hours (I had politely declined an invite as I was too busy to investigate the platform properly). Was this invitation, members only club worth joining? Well, I have yet to find anything of value to me but I can see why some people might like it and use it to great effect. I do wonder whether the launch would have been so successful had everyone been given free access right from the start. The key was to create a sense of prize and value in a product that is essentially free to use.

Place – Distribution

"Place" is all about ensuring that a product is distributed / sold in the right places. Brands are driven to try and increase their distribution to as many stores as possible. The view is that more products on the shelf means greater exposure and greater exposure can lead to greater sales.

There is a problem with this approach, however. If a retailer has 10 stores and 80% of their sales are in 2 of them, do you want to be in the 8 locations that only account for 20% of sales? Or do you want to be in the top 2? The other challenge is down to stock holding. Getting listed in the 8 stores that only represent 20% of sales will mean the stock they hold will be slow moving. After the initial listing and the stock is purchased, sales are likely to be slow. The retailer may end up with pockets of stock that are affecting their "open to buy" (their ability to make further purchases of product). This means that the product will be consolidated into a smaller number of stores and the stock cleared through or returned.

Distribution, then is about making sure you have the RIGHT products in the RIGHT place to serve the needs of the customer. Weighted Distribution Analysis will help brands identify the key locations to target.

All Airports Are Not The Same

It is really important to re-emphasise that all airports really are different. They have a different passenger profiles drive, to name a few:

- Demographics
- Psychographics
- Destinations
- Carrier of choice
- Connections
- Reasons for travel
- Time of travel

All of these factors and more influence how people will spend at the airport and the level of their spending. For this reason, each location should be treated in isolation until you identify similar patterns in spend to enable you to form clusters.

Clusters by country is a fallacy. For example, despite the UK having over 10 airports, each airport generally has a different passenger profile and therefore spend profile. There are some similarities, however these may not apply to your brand. You will need to run analysis to establish which airports can be grouped in a cluster for your respective brands.

Getting In Front Of The Right Audience

We developed a piece of software in-house that can identify the perfect range for any given group of Destinations or Nationalities based on the rate of sales across a retailer's business. This, by default helps a retailer prioritise the products and brands to ensure maximum impact. This approach has been used to great effect several times.

Promotions & Activations?

What is a promotion?

A promotion is usually where a product or a brand is highlighted to encourage shoppers to spend more than they intended to. This leads to incremental sales (sales that the retailer did not expect). In reality, promotional sales tend to steal from the core category sales and so incremental growth can be subjective at the best of times.

A promotion might be one or more of the following:

- Monetary value off (i.e. Save $10)
- Percentage off (i.e. Save 10%)
- Gift With Purchase (i.e. a free trolley back when you spend over $X)
- Purchase With Purchase (i.e. Get Product X for $10 when you buy Product Y)
- Increased focus (i.e. merchandising on a high profile site like the front of store)

- Increased staffing (i.e. agency staffing)
- Tasting

These activities are normally funded by the brand who benefit from additional volumes. However, not all promotions will work effectively and brands and retailers alike can end up losing cash margin by running them. This means that the volume uplift is not great enough cover the discount in the selling price.

Despite the level of investment that goes into promotions, there is very little analysis evaluating the effectiveness of promotions. A dependency on them has developed over the years.

What is an Activation?

An activation is a little different to a promotion although a promotion is usually used in conjunction with an activation. An activation has a little theatre involved, it might be in the form of a pop-up shop. A pop-up shop is additional selling space outside of the main store that is usually branded. For example, there was a Jameson's Irish Whiskey pop up shop in Dublin Airport. It contained only Jameson Whiskey and shoppers could make a purchase from there. This allows the brand to really showcase their product in the way that they want to. It is often a brand building exercise. It promotes the brand to passers-by but then it also allows people to have a unique experience.

Pop up shops are expensive as it usually involves paying for the space. The shop then needs to be built to the specific standards that the airports require and meeting fire regulations etc. Given the complex nature, this can also be an expensive exercise. The shop will need staff (usually agency staff) that need to be trained on the product and how to sell it. As you can see, there is a lot of cost involved and so it would involve a lot of product to be sold to ensure that the investment is covered. Are those costs covered? Sometimes they are, sometimes they are not. It depends on the product, the volumes and the margins. Some brands see the pop up store as a living advert for their product to drive brand awareness and home market purchases.

In the past, I have seen a brand take over the entire trail from the point of drop off to the store. This means that all the signage was taken to promoting this one brand. The signage was simple and distinctive. On evaluating the sales data, it had clearly not registered with the travelling passenger and made little difference to the sales figures. That was an expensive mistake.

The key here, I believe, is that awareness does not necessarily drive action. There needs to be something more and this is where the pop-up shops and other activations step in. It becomes an experience; it becomes a form of entertainment or education.

An activation might be in the form of a pop-up display in the main store or the taking over of a promotional site. Promotional sites are 'nodes of interest' dotted through the store to draw people's attention and interest. It also gives the retailer the opportunity to temporarily sell some of their space in store and generate additional revenues. These areas are usually staffed and involve sampling to enable the shopper to try the product. Brands can often be very creative. One brand put a bath in the store whilst another made part of the store look like a jungle! I have even seen a ski lift in a store in Singapore. The creativity tries to create a curiosity in the shopper and that is the first step to starting a conversation with the shopper.

Why are promotions and activations used?

There are a variety of reasons for using promotions:

- To drive interest and footfall into the store
- To clear out stock of lines that will be discontinued

- To increase basket size (think of a multibuy). Some shoppers might want to buy one item but then see a 3 for 2 offer and decide to spend more
- Brands often encourage promotions to try and get shoppers to switch to their brand once the promotion has finished. This is a step to grow overall market share.
- To launch a new product or brand
- To enable shoppers to 'try before they buy'
- To increase volumes and reduce production costs. This is where a brand will try to boost volumes to reduce the cost per unit to produce the product. This in turn increases profitability across all sales.
- Brand building exercise by getting exposure to an international audience.

This list is not exhaustive but I am sure you will agree that there are a wide range of reasons for a product to go on promotion.

How are they used?

They are often deployed at peak times when there is the most traffic. For example, summer holidays and Christmas. The aim is to get exposure to the most passengers.

In other situations there may be a promotional site in store that lasts 3 weeks and then another brand may take the site. This is to done to keep the store looking fresh and to draw the attention of those that might be travelling frequently. This rotation also helps to ensure that the staff are kept fresh and keen. In sales data we have noticed that promotional sales can wane after about 6 weeks. Of course, this may be due to stock issues but promotions can often get tired. Some retailers look to change their promotions every 2 months and therefore have 6 promotional slots per year.

Do they work?

Yes and no.

Some promotions absolutely work and can drive incremental sales whilst others fail to get any response. There is also the issue of cannibalisation to consider. Cannibalisation is where share is stolen from another product. So, imagine you have Brand X and Brand Y on display. Brand X is on promotion and sales are £3000. Brand Y's sales for that period are £1000. The total sales are £4000. In the next promotional slot, nothing is on promotion and sales are £4000 (all other things being equal). In the 3rd promotional slot, Brand Y is on promotion. Brand X's sales are £1000 and Brand Y's sales are £3000 (with all other things being equal again). What this is showing is that total sales are not benefiting from the promotion, the sales are just moving from one brand to another. This is an example of cannibalisation.

The challenge within the industry is that promotions are rarely assessed and this means that money is being 'given away'. There is a dependency on promotions and a fear that if a category or a product does not have a promotion, sales will decline. I have yet to see this tested however. If you have proven the case either way, please do let me know!

The great thing about Travel Retail is that you can test things very quickly thanks to the volume of traffic that goes through the store. A retailer could switch off all promotions in a particular category for a week or 2 weeks and get a very quick read on how it would impact sales. From here, the retailer can experiment with this 'baseline' to see how effective promotions are and how many are needed.

At World Duty Free, one of my roles involved looking after promotional analysis. I covered all the core categories including Liquor, Confectionery, Beauty and Luxury. Over those 18 months I saw mixed results. Some promotions didn't even move the needle whilst others succeeded.

Linked to this was the analysis on Activations. As mentioned above, activations are often a significant financial investment. The analysis would follow the same path as that of promotional analysis.

Some Challenges To Promotions

Are promotions necessary? Particularly given that the "Duty Free" or "Tax Free" message suggests that the shopper is getting a saving anyway. Well, it is difficult to say definitively because no retailer to my knowledge has avoided running promotions altogether. I have seen it where retailers have used fewer promotions and this works really well. The reason for this is because the level of choice is rationalised. Instead of being bombarded with lots of options and having a lack of certainty about which is going to be right for the individual, promotional effectiveness is watered down.

Another consideration is what the promotions are doing for the brand itself. Do constant promotions devalue the brand? Is money being given away? Would people be buying anyway? Following the Test & Measure principle will help answer some of these questions.

5 Promotion Power Questions

Before running a promotion, it is important to ask 5 power questions to really understand the 'why' of the promotion. It is key to understand the answers to the following questions to focus on the intent and commerciality of the promotion. The Power Questions are as follows:

1. **What is the purpose of this promotion?**
    Why do you want the promotion? Is it to drive visibility and brand awareness? Is it to reduce your marginal costs? Is it to

clear out old stock? Are you just trying to block your competitors from having that space?

2. **What is the benefit to the customer?**

   Is this really driving value for the shopper? Is there a strong compelling reason to buy your product?

3. **Will it pay for itself?**

   Will the loss in revenue through discounting be offset by volume uplifts? Will this drive incremental sales and cash margin for the retailer and the brand?

4. **Will it grow the category?**

   Will this steal share or is it going to genuinely grow the category by driving incremental sales and new shoppers? These are key considerations as the retailer will not want to lost potential sales and margin through discounting. Any promotion should be about driving incremental sales not moving them around between the brands.

5. **Would you do this again?**

   Once the promotion has ended, it is important to understand whether you would do this promotion again. If you re-run through convenience or habit, the chances are you are losing money. Really look for ways to refine a promotion and optimise via mechanic, location or brand.

In summary, we need to make sure that promotions are making money. Right now, there is not enough being done to ensure that we are indeed maximising every shopper opportunity.

PART 7

RETAIL SPACE MANAGEMENT

Here is a quick exercise. Take a moment now to think about your home. It might be your main living space, your eating area, your kitchen or your bedrooms. Think about the furniture you have in there. How much furniture do you have? How is it set out? Where are the chairs in relation to the TV? Where is the fridge in relation to the cooker and the sink?

Imagine that you have the opportunity to redecorate your main living room. You are given a budget to go out and buy new sofa, TV, coffee table etc. How would you go about selecting the furniture for your new room? What is your decision-making process?

Activity

Note down all the items that you would need to buy for a completely new living room. Consider the factors you would take into consideration when buying (i.e. colour, fabric, design etc). Now, grab some paper. Sketch out the shape of the room and mark where the items will go.

Activity Review

Let's review your answers. I wonder if you started out by thinking about how much space you have available? When we set about transforming a room in the house, we usually (consciously or unconsciously) consider the size of the room and what will fit.

A good example might be a TV for the living room. You might want an all-singing, all dancing 80" TV but if you only have a small living room, this is going to be a big problem!

So, without really thinking too hard about your living space, you already instinctively make decisions about décor and furniture based on the size of the room you have.

Take a look at your sketch. Does it look like it is to scale? If you were to put all those items in the room, would they fit?

There are 2 key points here that should be considered:

1. Before we can make decisions about what to put in a room, we need to know its limitations (i.e. – how big is the space we are working with)
2. Scale is a key issue when planning space. This will influence the size and amount of furniture you can have in the room.

As demonstrated in the example above, unfortunately the principles and processes that we take to decorate or re-arrange the rooms in our homes do not always extend into the day job. If you are a buyer or category manager, do you consider the assortment and ask 'will the range fit?'. If you are manager in store, how many times have you seen new lines appear in store and wonder where you are going to put them?

Space Planning is an essential but often overlooked function within Retail. It is the small cog in any retail business that can pull together many functions through one common arena – space on the shop floor.

What Is Retail Space Management?

I would define Retail Space Management as:

"*Space management is the* **commercial function** *that facilitates* **inter-departmental collaboration** *to deliver amazing retail experiences for shoppers in a profitable way whilst ensuring the* **efficient & effective use of retailer space and resources**"

Essentially, whether a retailer is a small corner shop or a huge mega store, availability of space will always be a limiting factor. The amount of space you have will determine the:

- Number of categories you can have in store
- Amount of fixtures you can have in store
- Number of till points
- Number of customers you can handle at any given time
- Breadth of the offer
- Size of the Range
- Amount of stock you can hold
- Level of theatre you can have in store

The amount of available space will influence the retailer's strategy. It is crucial then that a retailer plans their space effectively. The lack of focus on space and the absence of a clear range plan leads to all sorts of issues that erode profitability and the capability of a retail business to respond to an ever-changing market.

Space planning has 2 core components:

- Macro Space Planning
- Micro Space Planning

These 2 components, although related, require different skill sets.

The easiest way to explain Macro Space Planning is to use another example. Imagine you have a room with a large open plan that needs to be zoned into a Kitchen, Dining Area and Living Room space.

- The role of a Macro Space Planner is to work out how much space each area has, the amount of carpet or flooring that is required, how much furniture can fit into the space and the best place for each item of furniture. If there were bookshelves, the Macro Space Planner would work out how many are required.
- The Micro Space Planner would be concerned with fitting books, CD's, DVD's and other items onto shelves of the bookcases.

Macro Space Planning

In Retail, Macro Space Planning is concerned with the big space concepts:

- Store layout
- Number of fixtures
- The number of bays
- The number of shelves
- The position of till points
- The distances between fixtures
- The flow of shoppers in the store
- Signposts
- Activations
- Line of sight
- Category & subcategory flow

Macro Space deals predominantly with the footprint of the retail environment. This is measured in terms of square feet or square metres. Macro space also deals with the measurement of shelf space, which acts as a guide for the Micro Space Planning team. The Macro Space team also takes into consideration:

- **Category Flow**

  In terms of Travel Retail, this deals with core categories (i.e. Liquor, Tobacco, Beauty etc). Once the size, position and flow of these categories have been determined, the next stage is to work on...

- **Fixtures (also known as Store Furniture)**

  Using the footprints as a guideline, the Macro Space team will work out the number of fixtures it can fit into a store, their position and their ability to direct the passenger around the store. A fantastic example of great layout (but also frustrating at times) design can be found in Ikea. The layout is designed in such a way that encourages the shopper to visit and shop in every department.

- **Sight Lines**

  A great Space Planner will think about the shopper journey from beginning to end. The key here is to consider sightlines. What will the shopper see at each stage of their journey through the store? An outstanding space planner will work with the designers and marketing team to design the experience completely – what should the shopper be seeing, feeling and sensing at each stage. The ability to create an emotional connection with the passenger is a great skill to have.

- **Accessibility**

  I have touched on this before but accessibility is very important, particularly within a travel retail environment. Consider for a moment the typical passenger in the departures lounge. They are likely to be short on time and carrying at least one bag and or a pull along case. Those with children may have a pushchair to contend with. Someone who is disabled may have a wheelchair. If the store is to be accessible, the layout MUST enable 2 people with bags or pushchair to pass one another in an aisle. This means the fixtures must be at the very least 1.2 metres apart (4ft) or better still 1.5 metres apart (5ft). Remember – if they cannot access the store – they are less likely to shop. I have actually seen a store where determined shoppers actually left their pull along bags on the concourse to enter a store. Not ideal from a shopper perspective or for airport authority!

- **Hot Spots**
  Hot spots (areas in the store which have the most footfall) can often a topic of hot debate amongst retailers and brands but there is a simple way of predicting where a hot spot will be in store.

- **Passenger Flow**
  Macro Space planners will review the flow into and around the store. In an airport example:

  - Where do passengers come through security?
  - Where are the Flight Information Screens?
  - Where are the facilities (i.e. toilets, cash points, support desks etc)
  - Which Food & Beverage outlets are key and where can they be found?
  - How do passengers pass the store?
  - Where is their most likely point of access?
  - How do we want the shopper to enter the store?
  - How should we direct them once in the store?
  - How should they queue to pay and where?

There are more considerations that a macro space planner will have to weigh up including:

- What is the strategy for this location?

- Does Category X have enough Wall Space?
- Does Category Y have the visibility it needs from the front of store?
- How will I create an effective solution with the pillars?
- Will I fit all the Beauty brands in? Where will their personalised fixtures go?
- How will the shoppers flow through the store?
- How can we encourage cross selling with this format?
- What rule sets are in place for this store?
- How high can the Gondolas be?
- Do I need power for each fixture?
- How tall are my shoppers and will they be able to reach the product?
- What are the restrictions in place? (if any)
- How much shelf space will the layout create?
- Is that enough for the category?
- Will the range fit?
- Will the range have a credible representation?
- How many personalisation's (manufacturer fixtures) will be going in there?
- Which rule will you follow with regards to distances between fixtures
- Where do you want your brand signposts?
- How many till points do you need in store?
- Where will the till points go?

Micro Space Planning

Micro Space Planning relates to the small space concepts. It deals with the following:

- Segmentation
- Arrangement on shelf
- Assortment / Range

- Number of product facings
- Stock cover / Levels

If we go back to our room analogy and consider the bookcases, a micro planner will look to answer the following questions:

- How many shelves should have books? And how many should have CD's?
- Should the books go at the top or the bottom?
- How should those items be arranged?
- Should the books be in alphabetical order or grouped by subject?
- Should books be put in height order?
- Should the items be front facing, spine facing or lie flat and stacked?

In Retail, the Micro Space planner will create a plan for the operations teams to follow. That plan is called a Planogram. A planogram is essentially a map that tells the replenisher where each product should go and in what quantity.

The Micro Space function deals with product. They decide how best to position and merchandise product on shelf. Generally, they will follow the old saying that is 'The Eye Line Is The Buy Line' when merchandising. The highly effective micro planner's role is quite a broad one with a vast array of considerations to manage including:

- Recent sales trends
- Sales forecasts
- Category Strategy
- Merchandising rule sets
- Stock Requirements
- Promotions
- Range sizes
- Fixture dimensions
- Product Dimensions

- Space Productivity
- Reporting

The planner should have a close relationship with their key stakeholders. These stakeholders include:

- Macro Space Planners
- Buyers / Category Managers
- Marketing
- Retail Operations
- Suppliers

These planners will take the range plan for a store or a cluster of stores and create a solution that best represents the category ambitions.

In some cases, the Micro Space Planning will be completed in conjunction with a Category Captain. A Category Captain is a manufacturer with the resources available to be able to support the retailer by creating planograms for them. This does have its advantages including:

- Reduced Overhead Costs
- Plans are completed by people with in-depth knowledge of the category
- Low set up costs

However, there can be some challenges to this including:

- Biased planograms - the manufacturer providing the service may get preferential positioning and ranging in store even when the sales performances may not warrant it.
- Poor stakeholder management as the plans are usually completed off site.
- Detailed SKU Level Sales data needs to be shared with the manufacturer for all brands

One alternative is to utilise an independent third party to develop planograms. This would normally be in the form of an "implant" – someone who works for the consultancy but goes to work every day at the retailer. The Category Captain funds the role but also has shared access to this resource and provides support wherever possible in terms of product knowledge and product training etc. The key here is the fact that the Micro Space planner is independent. This means that although they have full access to the retailer data, they do not share the data with the Category Captain. This means that the retailer gets the best skill set, paid for by the Category Captain and is comforted in the knowledge that their data is secure. This also ensures that the right internal relationships within the business are maintained and the support is far more successful than if it had been undertaken by the manufacturer themselves.

The Link Between Macro Space and Micro Space

Macro and Micro Space presents a chicken and egg situation. How much space should be allocated to a category (i.e. Liquor)? If the Macro function works in isolation and allocates space based on return per square metre, the category (in this situation Liquor) may find itself with too little space to trade effectively. If the Micro function works in isolation, they will work with the space provided and not present constructive challenge to the Macro planners.

Essentially, space planning should be a collaborative function. If working correctly, it is the cog in the retail mechanics that can get all the functions in a business working together and in sync. This means that the buyers, supply chain, marketing can work efficiently and effectively to deliver the greatest return on space.

It is worth noting that for some reason, Micro Space planners and Macro Space planners (at the time of writing) rarely mix! It is incredibly rare to find people who have strong experience in both disciplines of Space Planning. One possible reason is that despite the fact these two elements are inextricably linked, Macro and Micro require a very different way of thinking.

Macro and Micro require a very different skill set and there is often very little overlap. There is of course areas where there are commonalities including:

- Attention to detail
- Operational considerations
- Stakeholder management
- Organisational skills

Why People Resist Space Planning

There are a number of reasons why key stakeholders will resist a Space Planning function. The key issue is that people think that Space Planning is restrictive. It is after all the Retail Police.

	Challenge	Reality
Front Line Retail	Many people who work on the front line like to 'play' with shops. They like to make changes and re-lay stores as they see fit. Others will 'squeeze' products in or position products based on gut feel.	Space Planning is based on analysis, research and psychology. It is there to make life easier for the front line teams so they can focus on what they should be doing – selling!
Replenishment Teams	Replenishers are often geared towards speed. They want to clear product off the cages and onto the shelves as quickly as possible. Having to follow a plan is seen as time consuming. For them, it is often	The planograms are based on analysis, strategic needs of the business and profitability targets. Accurate compliance of planograms will ensure that true productivity levels can

	perceived as something that blocks them doing their job quickly and effectively.	be assessed and future plans are adapted accordingly. This then impacts ranging decisions, stock purchasing etc.
Buyers	Buyers LOVE to add new products into store. They often send a stream of new lines in without any consideration of whether there is actual space within the store to fit them. They often become confused when sales targets are not achieved. Confusion often arises in terms of space productivity when comparing across categories. People often believe that higher productivity categories should command more space.	Space Planning ensures that the right number of products are in store. This prevents stock-outs, stock being kept in the store stock room and limits lost sales. Space planning will maximise every sales opportunity. Higher space productivity is not an automatic driver of space changes at a macro or a micro level. Using a strong space planning analyst is essential.
Marketing Teams	Marketing see space planning as restrictive at times. They want to be able to do their activities when and where they want. This can often cause confusion for multiple stakeholders and conflict within the categories.	Space Planning can hold an accurate record of the fixtures and the types of POS that can be used. This makes the Marketing team's job easier in the long term by creating simplicity.

Why Is Space Planning Needed?

Space Planning is critical in today's retail environment. This is even more critical in locations such as airports and cruise ships where space is often at a premium. Having a definitive plan can bring significant benefits.

There is a wide array of areas where Space Planning can have an influence:

- Range or Assortment size
- Store Developments
- Brand Positioning
- Till positioning
- Cross Category Merchandising
- Display quantities
- Stock levels
- Stock efficiency
- Return on Stock Investment
- Profitability
- Marketing & Signage and Point of Sale

Most parts of a retail business will interact directly or indirectly with a well-established Space Planning department. It is the one function that can bring people and projects together.

By tracking changes in Space, even at a Macro level, you can start to understand the effectiveness of each zone in the store. It helps retailers to identify which fixtures are the best, how shoppers are influenced by changes and therefore what can be done in the future to maximise performance.

Benefits of Space Planning

There are 2 key benefits of Space Planning:

- Operational
- Commercial

Operationally, Space Planning is the little cog that gets all the departments running in sync. Let us consider these examples and scenarios:

Marketing

Space Planning can supply details of store fixtures and fittings to help the marketing team plan the POS and light box requirements. They can work with the marketing team to plan the best location for activations and promotions. The Space Planning team can also support the marketing team in supplying dimensions and parameters for the creative agencies to work with.

Buying & Category Management

Space Planning can help the buying team to identify how much space their categories have in store, the location of that space, provide a guideline as to how much stock and how big a range will fit into the store. Space planning can also advise on space changes in order to deliver the best return on stock investment.

Supply Chain

When using planograms, the micro space planning team can work with the Supply Chain team to set the Min Max quantities for a store based on expected sales and space available. This helps the supply chain team maintain availability of key product lines to avoid lost sales. Some planogram systems can feed directly into the supply chain system so if you make a change to the planogram (i.e. double the facings of a particular perfume) it will tell the supply chain to send additional stock to the store to cope with the change in space.

Design and Development

The macro space team can advise on the best layout and create options to then be taken on by the designers for working into final concept drawings and set up. The macro space team can also help with the organisation of store developments by creating temporary layouts that the construction team can use during the re-fit. A well organised store re-fit will ensure that the store will minimise the impact on sales during a store reconfiguration or refresh.

Space planning also delivers commercial benefits. Retail space costs money. Whether you are paying a fixed rent or a concession fee structure (rent based or as a percentage of sales), it needs to be paid. If you invest each month for a position in a premium location, it is important that you generate a good return on your investment.

On top of the concession fee there will be heat, light, staffing, design and build…. the list goes on. Critically, the retail space needs to have stock on the shelves which ties up cash. Add too much stock of each product on the shelves and you impair your ability to operate efficiently, too little and you risk losing sales.

Tying up cash in stock means that the money cannot be invested in other parts of the business which can generate a return. For example, imagine you have $1m held in stock which could be released into other investments. If you have a project or an investment that could return a CAGR (compound annual growth rate) of 10%, that investment would be worth $1.6m at the end of 5 years. If you are holding it in stock, that money cannot work for you.

I once reviewed the retail space of a store and found that its AVERAGE stock holding of a high value category was 135 days cover! (Note: Days Cover is the number of days your stock would last at the average rate of sale. For example, if you had 50 units in store and you sold an average of 10 units per day, you would have 5 Days Cover). The store could have halved its stock holding and still maintained the current level of sales. Smart merchandising in store would have created an effective and engaging display that would have generated interest and conversion.

Space Planning, if done properly will deliver the following benefits:

- Better shopping experience
- Potential for increased sales
- Reduced Out Of Stocks
- Increased productivity
- Better return on stock investment (Gross Margin Return on Inventory Investment GMROII)
- Better Assortment Decisions
- Improved internal communication
- Better negotiation position for the buyers
- Better insight from the shop floor
- Identification of hotspots (zones in store with high footfall / sales)
- Increased cash margin

Key Learning Points

- Macro space deals with the big picture
- Micro space deals with the shelf detail
- Macro and Micro require different skill sets and having the ability to do both is rare.
- Space Planning is the small cog that can bring departments together
- Space is limited so use it wisely!

How To Set Up A Macro Space Function

Getting a Macro Space function is a relatively quick and easy process. It involves:

- Capturing the store layout (ideally use a technical drawing in software like AutoCAD)
- Deciding as to what level of space detail you want (usually to Subcategory level)
- Decide on the level of accuracy you need
- Measure the shelf space
- Capture the data into a database (even a spreadsheet will do)
- Audit on a regular basis (i.e. Monthly)
- Combine the space data with sales data to get productivity reports

If you have a floor plan you can usually capture a large store in a couple of days. The first capture is the part that takes the time. When you go to audit the store next time, the hard work has been completed and it is just confirming if anything has changed. If it has, capture that change. Audits are actually very quick.

Where Macro Space Planning really starts to add value is once you have built up a history of the data changes, particularly when promotion sites and activation sites have changed. Movement and change is the key to understanding space.

Measuring Macro Space

There are 4 key approaches to measuring retail space:

- Square Metres
- Linear Frontage
- Linear Actual
- Cubic Space

These approaches have their own merits which make them preferable for specific markets. The approaches are defined below:

Type	Explanation
Square Metres	This is the measurement of the footprint of the store. An example of this is where the length of a shop is 10m and its width is 30m. 10 x30 = 300 Square Metres.
Linear Frontage	This is particularly useful in locations where fixtures are standardised in size. This is often seen in supermarkets where all the fixtures have a standard dimension. If the bay is 1m wide, the Linear Frontage is therefore 1m. This is different to Actual Linear.
Actual Linear	Actual Linear is where the actual length of the shelves are measured. In this instance, a gondola end may be 1m wide and has 4 shelves. The Actual Linear space would be 4m. This is different to Linear Frontage which would have allocated space as 1m.
Aerial / Cubic	This is the amount of 3D space that is taken up by the products. This factors in the width, depth and height. This may be a used in other contexts or situations such as space used within delivery trucks.

Square Metres

Macro Space will always use Square Metres to evaluate the footprint of the store. If you are going to lay carpet, square metres is the measurement the carpet shop will want to know. In retail, you will need the store technical drawings to calculate square metres. Software such as AutoCAD will enable this. As well as capturing the total store, it is worth identifying how much space has been allocated to the core categories (Liquor, Tobacco, Confectionery, Beauty, Luxury). It would be too difficult to go to subcategories.

Square Metres is a number that requires context, particularly in Travel Retail. A relatively small square metre section of a store may contain a lot of wall bays and therefore the shelf density is higher. In contrast, there may be an area of the store with a large footprint but fewer wall bays and therefore shelving.

Linear Frontage

This approach measures the width of a bay on a fixture only. This approach is ideal when your store is highly standardised (i.e. a supermarket) and all fixtures are the same in terms of height and width. This makes evaluating space and standardising planograms simple. Instead of creating lots of planograms, the retailer can create a small number of options and apply them to the space they have available in a given store. For example, Store A might need 1m of Confectionery space. The store planner reviews the Confectionery options (let's say a choice of 1m, 2m, 3m planograms) and selects a 2m bay and sends the planogram to the store. This approach lends itself well to Modular ranging.

Linear Frontage

1m

Advantages

The advantages of this approach are as follows:

- Fast capture of space
- Minimum maintenance
- Smaller numbers to deal with
- Simple Approach
- Works well if the retailer uses standardised fixtures and modular ranging

Disadvantages

The disadvantages of this approach are as follows:

- Difficult to split the space of a bay into categories and subcategories
- Does not take into consideration the height of the fixtures
- Does not take into consideration the number of shelves
- Leads to inaccurate space productivity numbers in some environments
- Difficult to make decisions based on this approach in Travel Retail

Conclusion

This approach to measuring retail space is very simple and straightforward to do. It is easy to cover a lot of ground in a short space of time. This means that a retail portfolio or estate can be captured very quickly.

This approach is a challenge within the Duty Free channel. This is because fixtures are rarely standardised. Go into any airport store and you will find an array of gondolas of different sizes and shapes. The lack of standardisation is also evident across a portfolio of stores. Quite often, a store will be re-fitted and new fixture types will be designed and built. The reasons for this complete re-design can include:

- The introduction of brand personalisations
- Local adaptations to suit the given market
- Variety of store shapes and layouts
- Continuous updating of the store 'look'

Linear Actual

This approach captures the ACTUAL shelf space – the physical amount of space that is available for product to sit on. This approach is much more suited to locations which have a variety of fixtures (i.e. airport stores). Capturing space in this way means that the retailer can get a much more accurate view of the store productivity at a total level but also by category and subcategory.

In the example below, the 1m wide bay has 3 shelves which equates to 3 linear metres of actual shelf space.

Linear Actual

3m

Advantages

The advantages are as follows:

- Easy for non-space planning stakeholders to understand and relate to
- Captures true useable space

- Easy to split by category and subcategory
- Helps micro space planners when creating plans
- Allows localisation of planograms
- Better space productivity information
- Makes space optimisation easier

Disadvantages

- Takes a little longer to set up
- Higher maintenance
- A risk of inaccuracy if the store changes (adding or removing shelving or fixtures) anything without informing Space Planning
- Fixture variety can make measurement a challenge

Conclusion

This approach is, if done correctly and maintained appropriately, the one that is most suited to the travel retail industry. The capture of physical shelf space allows better comparison of space performances and can give an indication of how efficiently the space is working. The biggest advantage comes when trying to optimise space. By having actual physical space numbers available, you can make optimisation more of a science rather than an art.

Another reason for using Actual Linear is down to fixture types. A 1m wide Wall Bay might hold 5 shelves and therefore the recorded space is 5m. A 1 metre wide gondola bay might only have 3 shelves. If Linear Frontage was being used, both would be assigned 1m of space. The wall bay however has 67% more space than the Gondola bay.

Despite the challenges of maintenance and the impact of poor communication, this approach is by far and away the best option for Travel Retail.

Aerial / Cubic Space

Finally, in the interest of covering the main methods, there is an argument to suggest that the depth of the shelves should be incorporated when evaluating space. This approach factors in the height, width and depth to create a cubic measurement. This gives an indication of shelf capacity from a stock perspective.

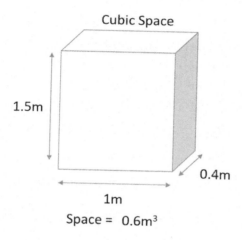

Cubic Space

1.5m

0.4m

1m

Space = 0.6m³

Advantages

The advantages of this are as follows:

- Indicate the amount of space available to hold stock
- Gives a true sense of physical space

Disadvantages

The disadvantages of this are as follows:

- Difficult for non-space planner stakeholders to relate to
- Cubic capacity number does not relate to physical shelf space
- Space capture takes longer
- Generates misleading space productivity information

Conclusion

This approach is not advisable for Travel Retail but has been included in the interest of providing options. A key challenge here is turning a number (such as the above – 0.6m^3) into a physical concept (i.e. Is there a large display area which has narrow shelves or a small area but with deep shelves?)

In Summary

The 4 key methods of capturing space have been reviewed and this presents a clear choice for space management in Travel Retail. The recommended approach is to capture Actual space. Although it will take slightly longer to do and will require a more controlled, centralised approach to making space changes in store, the benefits are clear:

- It will allow greater clarity and understanding for all stakeholders
- Improves dialogue between macro space planners and micro space planners
- Better space productivity information
- Space optimisation
- Effective hurdle rates for space changes

Which way is best?

Within Travel Retail, Space should be measured in two ways:

- Square Metres (or Feet)
  o Limited to the Core categories (Liquor, Tobacco, Confectionery, Beauty & Luxury (including watches, sunglasses, jewellery etc)
- Actual Linear Metres (or Feet)
  o Limited to a subcategory level (i.e. for Liquor Cognac, Whisky, Gin etc)

    ○   This is the most appropriate for Travel Retail due to the lack of standardization of fixtures.

    ○   It captures a true reflection of the merchandisable space.

Types of Fixtures

Now that the appropriate method of space capture has been selected (for Travel Retail it should be 'Actual'), a detailed look into measuring shelf space in store will be completed. Although this book cannot cover every type of fixture, it CAN give you the guidelines to effectively measure space within your stores and some simple rules to follow when approaching the task of measuring space.

The types of fixtures covered here include:

- Wall Bays & Gondolas
- Pillars, Promotional Stands & Free-Standing Display Units
- Curved Shelves
- Bulk Stacks
- Dump Bins
- Peg Boards

Based on the previous section, the measurement of Wall Bays and Gondola's are relatively straight forward. This chapter will cover common challenges for a space planner when the fixture might have a variety of configurations.

Shelf Configuration

This section deals with alternative shelf configurations and how the merchandisable space should be captured.

Split Shelves

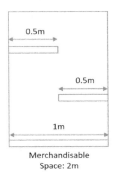

Merchandisable
Space: 2m

Here we see that a bay has shelving which is split for the purposes of creating an eye-catching display. This type of set up is more common in a category such as Beauty rather than Liquor or Tobacco.

The diagram is showing a bay that is 1m wide. The bottom shelf is 1m and the half shelves are 0.5m in distance.

1m + 0.5m + 0.5m = 2m of merchandisable space.

Light Boxes & Other 'On Bay' Furniture

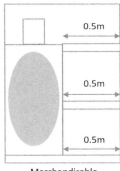

Merchandisable
Space: 1.5m

Some retailers will use light boxes or other cabinets to draw attention to a display or a gondola end.

The bay has half of its display taken over by a light box. On top of the light box is a show card which has details of a promotion on it.

The merchandisable space is on the right-hand side of the bay and is made up of 3 shelves which are 0.5m wide.

0.5m + 0.5m + 0.5m = 1.5m of merchandisable space.

Irrespective of whether the light box is permanent, at the point of capture, there is only 1.5m of shelf space available to be able to merchandise product. If the light box was removed at a later date and replaced with shelves, the space would then change. The space could then be re-audited and a new measurement would be captured.

Pillars, Promotional Stands and Free Standing Display Units

This type of fixture is common in airport stores and capturing the space often leads to a common mistake. Imagine for a moment that you are looking at a pillar with stock on all four sides. Each side is 1m wide. The pillar has 5 shelves on each side.

A simple approach would be to say:

1m x 5 = 5m for each side.

5m x 4 sides = 20m of merchandisable space. Right? Wrong!

If we look at this approach in the image below in Option 1, you will see in the bottom left-hand corner a shaded area. This shaded area represents a problem. Double counting. If you think about bottles of Vodka on the shelf, although one side you will see the front of the bottles, the other side you will see the sides of the bottles.

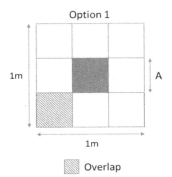

Option 1

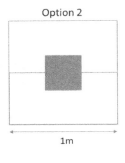

Option 2

Overlap

The correct way to measure this space is Option 2 which treats it like a double-sided fixture. This means that the following calculation is made:

1m x 5 = 5m

5m x 2 sides = 10m of merchandisable space

Here we see that the duplication is removed and space can be captured accurately.

There is one caveat to this principle. The space 'A' highlighted in Option 1. If this space is large enough to hold different product, capture it as merchandisable space.

In this instance, let us assume that 'A' is 0.5m wide.

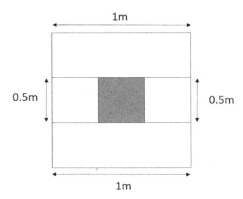

The calculation would be as follows:

1m x 5 = 5m

5m x 2 = 10m

PLUS the additional side displays....

0.5m x 5 shelves = 2.5m

2.5m x 2 sides = 5m

10m + 5m = 15m of merchandisable space.

These principles hold true for a Pillars, Promotional Stands and Free-Standing Display Units.

Curved Display Units

This is one type of display that causes confusion when it comes to measuring the space. For this reason, keep it simple! Measure the straightest line. An example of this might be circular promotional stands. In this instance, measure the diameter of the fixture, multiply it by the number of shelves and then multiply it by 2. If you have a circular stand which is 0.75m wide and has 3 shelves the calculation would be:

0.75m x 3 shelves x 2 sides = 4.5m of shelf space.

Bulk Stacks

With regards to bulk stacks, a company-wide decision must be taken regarding space assigned. This could be a generic quantity, regardless of the format of product. An example might be 5m. This makes the assumption that if you put all the stock from the bulk stack onto shelves, it would probably take up the space of one wall bay (usually 5 shelves at 1m wide).

Whatever your company decides, this rule should be captured and documented so that all parties are clear and understand the implications.

Dump Bins

Dump bins are usually put near the till or in impulse locations around the store. A similar approach to Bulk Stacks should be taken. Create a standardised space for them (i.e. 3m) and this is used regardless of the category.

Peg Boards

This is a bay where you put hooks into the back board and hang product off the hooks. This is a difficult one to specify and judgement will come into play. Imagine then, for a moment, that on the side of a 1m wide bay there are 6 rows of printer cartridges. Because of the format of this fixture, the easiest approach is to multiply the number of rows by the width of the bay:

1m x 6 rows = 6m of merchandisable space

The reason for this approach is because if you sat the items on a shelf, you would need 6m of shelving to do so. When you have mixed subcategories hanging in one bay (i.e. power adaptors and batteries), use best judgement based on the principles set out.

Accuracy

Measuring space can be as easy or as complicated as you want to make it. The degree of accuracy will be dependent on who will be using the space information.

If you are planning on capturing the macro data for micro space planners to use, measurements to the nearest millimetre must be taken. Take this example:

A macro space planner audits a store and decides that a bay has shelves that are 1 metre wide. In reality, the shelves are 0.95 metres wide. This is a difference of 5 centimetres. The space planner creates the plan and sends it to the store. The store finds that the products do not fit on the shelf correctly and dismiss the planogram as a whole. This causes internal problems and a lack of faith or belief in the power of effective space management. The knock-on effect is that the supply chain may have set up your MDQ's (minimum display quantities) incorrectly and this leads to incorrect stock being sent. This could lead to lost sales, a to stock room filling up, and warehouse staff on the shop floor at inappropriate times which in turn makes it difficult for the shoppers to buy product.

Ideally, technical drawings would be sourced to make the process much easier to do. This allows the space planner to see the size of the fixtures, the notch heights (so they can make decisions on shelf heights), shelf depths etc.

If you only operate a Macro space planning department, the need for millimetre accuracy is not necessary which in turn can speed the process up. If a bay is indeed 0.95 metres wide, capturing it as 1 metre is forgivable. All parties will need to agree that a zone of tolerance is required.

Capturing Space Information On A Floor Plan

Capturing the space and category information in the right way makes it easy to evaluate a layout at a glance. When you capture space, it is critical to try and capture it at the same levels as your product hierarchy. For example, if your Tobacco category contains Cigarettes, Cigars, Roll Your Own and Accessories, you should capture your space to the same level. This will make space productivity reporting easier.

Below is an example of a fixture that you might find on a store layout. The layout has had notes added to it by bay.

		American 3	Irish 3		
Scotch 3	PROMO				Scotch 3
		Scotch 3	Scotch 4 (Half bottles)		

(Note: This is an example only and not a recommendation).

On this plan, it is easy to see:

- That this is a Liquor Gondola
- The breakdown of space by sub category
- The actual space by bay
- The Promotion bay which also indicates likely flow

In addition to the above, there is a note to say that one of the bays is made up of half-bottles. This explains the additional shelf (assuming that each bay is 1m wide). You can also label each fixture and bay with a specific Fixture ID and Bay ID. This helps with tracking changes though it does slow down the audit process.

This simple 2D plan contains a great deal of information. If software such as AutoCAD is being used, additional 'layers' can be used for additional notation (i.e. bay numbers, fixture types, photo's etc). Premium versions of AutoCAD can also be set up to extract the space data automatically and put it into a database for analysis to remove the need for manually counting space.

Additional supporting information is useful to capture including the distances between pinch points. A pinch point is the narrowest point between 2 or more fixtures. This helps with the evaluation stage of a layout or when considering a re-fit.

Many types of stakeholders can easily use this format to understand what is in store. For example, a buyer can read this layout and see that there is 3m of space available to American Whiskies and can therefore plan the range appropriately.

How often should the space be audited?

This will vary significantly depending on the support you have from your stakeholders (category team, retail operations, supply chain etc). If the retailer has strict centralised control over space and creates planograms, a quarterly space audit may be enough. Most retailers within Travel Retail do not have this level of centralised control and therefore a more frequent approach to space audits is recommended. A monthly store audit should be appropriate.

Given the nature of Travel Retail; the fact that the store portfolio can be widespread, there may be an impact on the audit process and frequency.

Who should audit the stores?

Ideally, the stores should be audited by the Macro Space Planner. The reason for this recommendation is that a highly effective space planner will not just audit the store. The individual will be:

- Assessing customer flow
- Talking to staff and getting feedback on operational aspects
- Reviewing weaknesses and pinch points (areas where bottlenecks and congestion can appear).
- Shopping behaviours
- Selling to passengers
- Talking to passengers to get feedback and views
- Reviewing the detail – spot checking planogram compliance

The planner will factor all of these points into their future layouts and store designs when it is time to do a store development or departmental re-lay.

Where this is not possible (e.g. the cost of flying a space planner to a specific store is too cost prohibitive), an individual from the store should be trained and seconded to capture store space once per month. The individual should be:

- Fully trained by the space planning team
- Supplied a current floor plan
- Provided facilities to update space changes electronically
- Able to scan their notated floor plan and email across to the space planner for further discussion
- Able to send photo's to support changes made

How Long Should Audits Take?

An audit, once everything has been set up for the first time, is likely to take a couple of hours (depending on the size of the store that needs to be captured and the amount of changes made). The audit should be set in stone (i.e. the store will be audited on the first Wednesday every month) and the individual should not be taken away from that task.

This might seem like an odd comment to put in this book but Trust is a significant factor here. There MUST be a level of trust in place between the space planning department and the seconded individual. It is essential for the Space Planning department to have accurate plans and that the audit has indeed been completed. The seconded auditor must not just sign off the plan and say 'yeah yeah, I did it, it's still the same as last month'. This would lead to:

- Inaccurate floor plans
- Inaccurate planograms
- Poor reporting (Garbage In, Garbage Out as they say)
- Poor decision making regarding future space
- Poor credibility

However you decide to audit your stores and maintain the plans that you have, consistency and accuracy are key to ensuring that the department remains effective.

Example – A Store Relay

I was once asked to review a layout of an satellite store. The sales performance had been in continuous decline year on year for the previous 12 months. Many had reviewed the store and made changes but failed to turn the performance around. Having reviewed the sales data, I did the most valuable thing a space planner can do, I sat outside the shop and watched. Over the space of a couple of hours during peak flow, I formulated a plan that would prove to deliver the turnaround performance. There is no substitute for getting out to store with a cup of tea and a notepad. Filming studies do have their uses but the statistics they generate do not always uncover the solutions. What you are looking for is the tiny almost imperceptible shifts in gesture and body language as the passenger goes about their business.

The key to success was in the position of the fixtures. The existing angle of the fixtures created a barrier to entry. The new plan had to harness the passenger's line of sight and encouraged shoppers to cross the threshold of the store.

Once the store had been changed, I sat in the airport and watched again. I could see the change in behaviour instantly. Now the passengers were not being deflected, there was an increase in the number of people who had actually entered the store without realising it. They had been so caught up in looking into the store. This led to one final and subtle change to the angle of some of the fixtures in store so that shoppers had to go deeper into the store in order to get out. This led to an increase in impulse purchasing. The new layout, combined with a smarter approach to the ranging (the precursor of ranging by destination) enabled the store to reverse its fortunes and achieve a growth of +8% year on year and it continued gaining momentum.

Example 2 – Scaling Drawings

I once worked with a category manager who sketched out on paper:

- How they wanted the layout to look in store
- The number of fixtures they required
- The brands they wanted and their position

Having spent many years designing layouts in stores, I could see that there was going to be a potential issue. I sourced a technical drawing and created the proposed layout. Whilst it was a great idea to sketch out the concept, the technical drawing highlighted that there were far too many fixtures and that passengers would not be able to fit between them in some cases. This led to a complete re-think of the store. By utilising a space planning resource, the retailer saved a significant amount of time and cost. Had they proceeded with the layout change, they would have realised the constraints they had and would have needed to think fast to create a suitable layout before the store opened again. This is neither efficient nor effective. Operationally, there would also be the issue of stock listing, distribution, stock holding etc. to contend with. Had new brands been introduced, the retailer could have been sat on stock that they could not put into store.

SETTING UP A MICRO SPACE FUNCTION

At Dixons Group, I was part of a team that set up a Macro Space Planning department from scratch for the Currys chain.

At WDF I had to set up the Micro Space Planning department from scratch. This meant that I had to measure every shelf, every product and evaluate sales. In some respects it was a steep learning curve for me as Travel Retail is different to domestic retail in many ways.

I remember that I had the challenge of measuring every single Liquor product within the business. At the time, WDF had something called a Cubiscanner. The idea is that you place a Products on this machine and an arm would scan the products and capture the dimensions. I was assured that this was the right thing to do. This was in theory, a great idea. I stood in freezing cold warehouse with a never-ending trolley of products putting them on and measuring them. After about 100 products I did some random checks and realised that the machine made the product wobble when the measuring arm moved. Because the product wobbled, the measurements that the scanner was taking were inaccurate. This meant that I had to measure all of the products again using calipers. Remember this was in a freezing cold warehouse.

It might seem like a sensible idea to contact the suppliers for dimensions. However, this was a problem as suppliers were not always quick to come back with the dimensions I needed or the dimensions were not available. This meant I had no other choice but to measure the products manually. In the Liquor category alone, this meant I needed to measure well over 500 products. The next step was to measure the fixtures.

A trial store was selected and every fixture had to be measured. This requires a broad selection of dimensions to be captured. To create a planogram affectively, you need to be able to access fixture height, fixture widths, shelf depths, thickness of the shelves, notch heights and more. When it comes to taking dimensions, you must remember that they will need to be millimetre specific.

Unfortunately, there are no shortcuts and no generalisations are available. Imagine you have bay that is 1m (1000mm) wide. If you assume that the bottles are 100 mm wide, it means you can get 10 bottles across on that shelf. However, if your bottles are actually 103 mm wide you'll find that You cannot fit 10 bottles wide. Because the measurement of the bottle is incorrect by 3 mm it means that you can only fit nine bottles on the shelf.

This also has implications for depth a shelf too. How much stock can you actually fit on the shelf if you have not taken the measurements of the product correctly? This is one of the biggest challenges a Micro space planner faces. If you design a planogram and it doesn't fit, this can cause an operational problem. And the person in store whose job it is to implement the planogram is the one faced with the problem. What should they do? Should say just fit nine products on the shelf and put the rest in the stockroom? Or should they redesign the plan themselves and come up with their own planogram? If retail operations do not trust planogram is in the first instance, they will reject any future planograms.

Space planning can often be seen as a problematic department. The reason for this, I believe, is that many functions see this department as being an obstacle. Space planning can actually be the small cog that allows everything to work together in a highly effective way.

Remember. Stores do not have rubber shelves.

Efficient and effective retail requires strict discipline and control when it comes to defining processes to manage assortment and space.

Reviewing space leads to big questions such as:

- What is the optimum assortment size?
- How much space should I allocate by category?
- How should I layout my store for the maximum effect on the shopper?
- What can I do to maximise every shopper journey through the store?

These types of questions transform the retail conversation towards the shopper needs and how to execute against those needs.

Creating the Product Library

A product library is a database with all the product information you need to be able to create planograms. This can seem like a daunting task. Once complete however, it is relatively straightforward to maintain. The key components of a good product library are:

- Product Dimensions
- Product photos
- Product Information (i.e. special notes in terms of how to display etc)

When capturing dimensions, there is no substitute for getting a set of callipers to take millimetre accurate dimensions. Some will tell you that the quickest way of getting dimensions will be source them from the manufacturers. It sounds like a straightforward idea, however, think about the number of brands and manufacturers the retailer deals with. Sourcing accurate data quickly is a challenge.

If you want accurate product information, get the space planner into the warehouse and do the measuring with actual product. It might seem like a time-consuming challenge but it really is a worthwhile investment.

Building Planograms

When building planograms, there are other factors or rules which need to be taken into account. These rules are simple and worth keeping in mind when managing space. Ask yourself the following questions:

- What are the minimum number of facings a product should have?
- How many days cover should I have on shelf?
- What is the minimum case quantity that should be put on shelf?

These 3 questions are ESSENTIAL in order for a retailer to have highly effective and efficient retail space. The reasons for this are as follows:

What are the minimum number of facings a product should have?

This is key and will vary by category. If you are selling books for example, single facings may be acceptable but in some categories this may not be appropriate. If you are going to sell a product, you might as well give it the proper representation it deserves. Different categories will require a different number of facings and this should be decided as a business. As a general guideline, 2 to 3 facings is a good number to have in Travel Retail. It gives the product enough space to be perceived to be credible.

How many days cover should I have on shelf?

If you are going to sell a product, you need to ensure that you have got enough stock to cover the rate of sales. If you are continuously selling through and going out of stock, you have lost sales, a gap on shelf and your reputation as a retailer has been impacted. In Travel Retail, you have one opportunity to get it right because in an hour or so they will be on a plane and lost forever.

Imagine that you have given a Liquor product 3 facings. On a typical Liquor shelf you can get 4 bottles deep. This means that you have 12 bottles on shelf. If you were able to sell 20 units per day, you have a problem unless you have a stock room on hand and someone ready to monitor and refill the shelves. This takes a person's attention off the customer and impacts sales. From a stock delivery perspective, you then have a problem with the frequency and efficiency of deliveries.

Another point to remember, if you have a large stock room with stock in it, the stock room cannot be traded and therefore it is taking up potential selling space (assuming it is adjacent to the shop floor).

The point made about stock rooms leads nicely to the final question...

What is the minimum case quantity that should be put on shelf?

If you are seeking optimum efficiency in retail, you will need to consider removing the stock room altogether. The best-case scenario would be taking stock directly from delivery lorries to the shop floor. This means that the product is only handled once. Stock (unless you have individual stock picking in your warehouse) will normally be sent to store in its cases. For Spirits it is convenient and reduces breakages or damage. If you receive a case to the store, you will want that to go straight onto the shelf. A minimum stock holding on shelf might therefore be 1.5 to 1.7 cases.

If we go back to the scenario in the previous point – we have suggested that the minimum facings should be 3. This means that with a typical depth of 4 bottles, you have a stock on shelf figure of 12 units (2 cases). If the case size is 6 bottles, this is absolutely fine. The shelf can be shopped and still look respectable by the time the replenishing case arrives. If, however, the case has 9 bottles in, this means that you could be left with less than 3 bottles on shelf by the time the new stock arrives and this makes the display look unappealing. This would therefore push your stock holding up to 14 units on shelf which would then require 4 facings. Once again, if the line is in the bottom 20% of sales value, it puts pressure on the space available.

OK. Time for a re-cap.

Space is fixed. It is an asset that incurs a cost (rent, heat, light, staffing etc). Maximising the return that you have on that space is critical. To maximise that return, you need to make that space as efficient as possible. To do this, you need to allocate the right amount of space to products. Allocating space based on percentage of sales value leads to an inefficient use of space, potential over stocks and lost sales.

To be truly efficient, you need to consider:

- Rate of sale (unit movement)
- How many days stock cover you should have on shelf.
- The minimum number of facings that you want to have.
- How many cases should be on shelf.

As you can see, there are interdependencies when looking to allocate space. Allocation of space based on % share of sales, is probably note the best approach.

Implementing Planograms

If a retailer is going to invest in the time to create a space planning function, it is important that the retailer also enforces compliance. This use of the word "enforce" may come across as a little harsh but it is a significant point and one that must be addressed.

Take a moment to think about the actual planogram. The micro planner has spent a significant amount of time liaising with key stakeholders across multiple functions, analysed sales data, reviewed sales forecasts and poured a significant amount experience and knowledge into creating a planogram for the store to implement. If this is not followed, all of the effort that has gone into creating the plan will have gone to waste. This could actually equate to hundreds of people hours and insight being thrown in the bin.

On the flip side, do micro space planners get it right every time? Of course not. I often joke that give 5 micro space planners a planogram to do and they will give you 5 very different plans. What is important is that when planograms are issued, a supporting methodology must also be issued. This does not need to be reams and reams of supporting notes – a few succinct bullet points to provide the rationale behind the plan e.g.:

Example Supporting Planogram Notes

The planograms contained within this pack have been created taken into account the following points:

1. The carrier profile of this store is predominantly low-cost airlines.
2. The flights are international short haul flights.
3. Key nationalities (X, Y, Z) have show a preference for buying brands (A, B, C)
4. A key volume driver is the lower price point in this store. The plan should encourage trade up.
5. Key promotional sites are maintained.
6. Supplier promotional fixtures have been accommodated and these planograms have been supplied by the manufacturer.
7. The planogram seeks to achieve:
   a. Clear 'good, better, best' principles
   b. Brands are clustered where appropriate.
   c. Product price logic is set as leading in with high price point.

d. All lines should have a minimum facings of 3 units.

8. If gaps appear, fill with the adjacent product. Revert back when stock comes in.

Providing notes like in the example above clearly shows the logic and thinking that has gone into creating the planogram. Without this, it is easy for retail operations or other stakeholders to be dismissive. The clear advantage of such a supporting document is that it facilitates active discussion.

The notes should be very much aligned to the category and retailer strategy. So, if the strategy of an airport retailer is to drive the growth of Malt Whisky, the planogram and space allocation (completed in conjunction with Macro Space Planning) will reflect the ambition of the category managers and the retailers.

How To Constructively Challenge A Planogram

Have issues with the planogram? Want to know how to challenge it? The key here is to remember that planograms are often subject to debate. If you want a change made to the planogram, first you need to establish the core reason for the change:

- Is it a physical issue? Products do not fit?
- Is it an opinion led request?

If it is a physical aspect such as the shelf heights, products not fitting etc, then the retailer and the space planning team should have a process to provide the feedback to do so. In theory, this should never happen if the products and the fixtures have been measured correctly! BUT, like everything, mistakes happen. Challenge of the planogram in this context should be very straightforward.

If the challenge is an opinion led, following the steps set out below will allow constructive challenge the space planner in a non-threatening, non-confrontational way:

- Be clear on what you would like to see changed and why it should be changed
    - Line X is constantly going out of stock on shelf, I need additional facings
    - I think we are missing out on link selling Category X when a shopper selects Category Y
    - I would like to see Brand F have better visibility because it is very popular with Nationality J
- Have evidence to support your case
    - Sales data
    - In-store Observations
    - Customer comments and feedback
    - In-store Photos
- Ask questions
    - I keep having stock issues on line X, what can we do with the planogram to change that?
    - We are seeing an increasing number of people cross selling themselves in store. How can we make it easier for the shopper to do this?
    - Can you talk me through the rationale of having Brand X here? (Remember, this might be space that the retailer has sold to a brand and therefore it is there for a commercial reason)
- If necessary, aim to agree a compromise
    - If we do this, can we monitor it and if necessary, look to change it in the next set of planograms
- Offer support
    - How can I help you deliver the change?
    - Is there anything you need from me to get this update completed?

Bottom line here is to make sure that you win hearts and minds. Most Micro Space Planners are amicable souls. If you have a strong case, persist but remember it might mean losing a few battles to win the war!

Space Productivity

Evaluating space productivity requires 2 key elements.

- A database of space with historical changes captured
- Sales data

To understand how productive space is, we need to match the sales to the space used for the duration. Space productivity reporting is normally done on a monthly basis. The analysis is normally run at a high level based on your internal product hierarchy.

In the table below, there is a fictitious store that demonstrates space productivity reporting for a given month:

Category	Space (Actual Linear metres)	Sales ($)	Sales / Mtr
Liquor	250	800,000	3,200
Tobacco	150	300,000	2,000
Confectionery	250	400,000	1,600
Total	650	1,500,000	2,308

Here we can see that across the 3 core categories, the most productive space is Liquor at $3,200 per metre. To some, it would mean that Liquor Space should be increased as this will make the overall space more productive. To others, there is a deeper story to be discovered.

The Variables

Let us take a moment to consider the elements that influence Space Productivity. Sales per Metre will be a result of sales divided by space. This number may be influenced by 2 key factors:

- a change in sales AND/OR
- a change in space.

It is important to point out that adding an extra 50m to Liquor will not necessarily generate an extra $160,000 of sales (50 x 3,200). It is more likely to reduce the productivity of Liquor to $2,667 per metre assuming all things remain constant.

The next step is to understand how much of an influence an extra 50m of space will have over the total sales. The questions that spring to mind here are:

- Is this 50m of new space? Or taken from another category?
- Are you doing more of the same?
- Are you adding new subcategories?
- Are you adding new sku's that appeal to a new audience?

All of these elements will have an influence.

Space Productivity is also influenced by position in store. If a category is moved from a 'cold area' to a more visible area, what would the effect be? Will sales increase? The chances are they would. The other factor to consider is that the effect on the displaced category.

How will moving to a poor visibility or cold area impact sales?

One approach to calculating the effect of such moves is to create a model such as the one below:

Category	-6%	-4%	-2%	0	+2%	+4%	+6%
Liquor	(48)	(32)	(16)	800	16	32	48
Tobacco	(24)	(16)	(8)	400	8	16	24
Confectionery	(18)	(12)	(6)	300	6	12	18

Imagine you want to move Liquor to a colder space and move Confectionery into the space given up by Liquor. If you believe that moving Liquor to a colder part of the store will cause sales to fall by 2%, the loss in sales will be -16k. If this is the case, Confectionery will need to increase by almost +6% to offset that loss in sales.

If you have a portfolio of stores, you may find that you can begin to predict the impact of sales by comparing locations and store positioning. Travel Retail adds a level of complexity to this analysis when you take into consideration the location passenger profile.

Comparisons and benchmarking CAN be made but they must be made with a degree of caution.

The perfect scenario is to build a history for the stores and compare performance over time. We encourage retail clients to "Test & Measure".

The Common Mistakes When Reviewing Space Productivity

Assuming An Increase In Space Will Increase Productivity

Let's think about this logically. All other things being equal when you increase space, assuming sales remain constant, space productivity falls. So, sales are $15,000 from a space of 250 ft. Space productivity is $60 / ft. If you double that space to 500 ft you will immediately see productivity drop by half to $30 / ft. To maintain the same level of productivity ($60), you would need to see sales double to $30,000. The lesson here is if you are going to focus on space productivity as a metric and you want to increase space, be sure to increase sales above and beyond the space growth.

Comparing Productivity Across Categories Without Context

Comparing space productivity across categories (i.e. Skin Care vs Vodka) is a non-starter. This gives you a false read on productivity because of the differing price points but also product size. You might be able to display a whole range of Brand X's skincare on a single bay of a gondola but need 3 wall bays to display Brand Y's Vodka. Essentially, comparing space productivity across categories isn't comparing apples with apples. The real analysis is in the detail.

Seeing All Stores Productivities As Comparative Without Context

Comparing the space productivity of a Main store vs a Satellite store does not really give a fair view. The productivity is likely to be much lower because the footfall into the store will be considerably lower. If space productivity is to be compared, make sure that you cluster your locations effective

Ignoring stock value

When reviewing space productivity, it is worth considering the amount of stock that is being held to support the rate of sale. This is an indication of efficient use of space.

The Importance of Assortment on Space Management

Assortment will of course have a huge influence over space productivity.

Ever heard of the Pareto Effect? This is also known as the 80/20 rule. When applied to retail, it suggests that 80% of sales are likely to come from 20% of the range. The chart below is based on live data where 80% of sales do indeed come from 20.8% of the range.

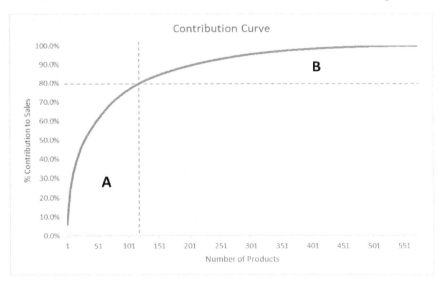

This is an interesting concept when you factor in space. Products in the Top 20% of Sales will require more space to support the rate of sale. However, the products in the Bottom 80% of sales (the tail) will require enough space to represent a credible offer (i.e. a minmum of

3 facings, supporting halo products etc). It is highly likely that the products in the bottom 10% of sales will be significantly over represented in terms of space.

So, we can conclude that WITHIN a category or subcategory, space productivity will vary. The space allocated to top performers is likely to be very productive whilst the tail is going to be increasingly less productive. Faster moving lines are likely to have more productive space compared to the very slow moving lines in the tail.

This is where the dark art of space productivity comes in. To explain, let us walk through an example.

Reallocating Space Scenario

A store is looking to reallocate some of its space. The store has a 6m of wall bay that represents 30m of actual shelf space. 25m of the shelf space is given to Beauty, 5m of shelf space is given to Confectionery.

Let's take a new example:

	Sales	Space (m)	$ / m
Beauty	$1,200	25	$48.00
Confectionery	$125	5	$25.00
Total	$1,325	30	$44.17

We can see that the Beauty is clearly more productive in terms of return per metre. What would you do? Give Beauty all of the space?

As a space planner, you speak to the store to get an understanding of what is going on. You find out that the Confectionery bay is having to constantly be replenished. The Confectionery Buyer also wants to introduce a new subcategory of healthy snacks and could do with more space.

You decide to dig into the detail a little more as you are aware that productivity diminishes as the range size increases. You find that the detail is as follows:

Bay	Space (ft)	Category	Sales ($)	$ / m
1	5	Beauty	500	100
2	5	Beauty	300	60
3	5	Beauty	250	50
4	5	Beauty	100	20
5	5	Beauty	50	10
6	5	Confectionery	125	25
-	30	**Total**	**1325**	**44.72**

Here we see that overall productivity is $44.72 per metre of shelf space. Beauty, although at a total level is operating at $48 per metre, within the category there are wide variations. Sales per metre of shelf space range from $100 to $10. With this visibility, we can see that Bays 4 and 5 are both less productive than Confectionery. This was hidden when we failed to consider the bay-by-bay space which is in turn driven by Assortment.

You meet with the Confectionery category manager and ask for their plan and forecast. They come back with the following:

- Recovery of lost sales due to stock outs is worth $50 per week
- Introducing the new category would be worth £75 per week
- The new category would need 3 shelves of a bay (each bay is made up of 5 x 3ft shelves)

If Confectionery had more space, it could double its sales from $125 to $250 per week.

If Bay 5 was taken from Beauty and those products were delisted, the cost to the Beauty category would be $50 per week. The potential gain from Confectionery is $125 so the move would deliver a net benefit of $75 per week. If you were able to flex the space of other slower moving beauty lines, you may still be able to keep the full Beauty range and not impact sales.

By digging into the detail of the assortment, a different space productivity story emerges. Where it seemed obvious to get rid of Confectionery from the wall bay, there is now good reason to extend it.

The actions would therefore be as follows:

- Condense the existing Beauty range
  - Review stock cover and reduce facings on over stocked lines where appropriate
  - Consider completing a range review to rationalise the range
- Give Bay 5 to Confectionery
  - The equivalent of 3 shelves would be given to the new category
  - The equivalent of 2 shelves would be given to the existing range to provide more support stock for faster moving lines.

Assuming the Beauty sales remain constant on less space, and the Confectionery category hits its forecast, the results would look like this:

Bay	Space (ft)	Category	Sales ($)	$ / Ft
1	5	Beauty	500	100
2	5	Beauty	300	60
3	5	Beauty	250	50

4	5	Beauty	150	30
5	5	Confectionery	125	25
6	5	Confectionery	125	25
-	**30**	**Total**	**1450**	**48.33**

Even if you did lose sales from the products on Beauty Bay 5, productivity would still be higher at $46.66.

The summary shows a change in category productivity:

Bay	Space (ft)	Category	Sales ($)	$ / Ft
-	20	Beauty	1200	60.00
-	10	Confectionery	250	25.00

The review of space performance at a deeper level identifies opportunities to work the space harder. In this instance, condensing Beauty into 4 bays increases overall space productivity of the category by $12 per metre of shelf space. The Confectionery category sales would increase as forecast and this would see the productivity remain constant. The overall effect on the space productivity would be as follows:

- Pre Change   - $44.72 / ft
- Post Change   - $48.33 / ft

Had Beauty been extended, Sales would have needed to go $1,440 (a 20% increase) to maintain space productivity levels.

On a side note, not only has the productivity of the store gone up but the value of stock held on the shop floor would have declined. This means that the store is getting a better return on stock investment.

Stock value is often overlooked in Travel Retail however, stock tied up in store or warehouses can impact the buying team's ability to buy.

Example: Factoring In Stock Value

In Travel Retail, there is a trend towards premiumisation on a large scale. Some retailers have chosen to turn stores over to a Super Premium experience. This provides a significant but hidden challenge. I can think of a retailer where they removed all entry-level lines from the store and filled it with very expensive super premium and exclusive lines. The shelving remained similar and so the amount of stock it held probably stayed about the same in terms of number of items. The new store traded and the despite significantly less footfall and conversion, the sales remained flat. This was considered a success by the retailer because they achieved the same level of sales through doing 'less work'.

If we review the detail, despite the higher price point, margin percentage is likely to have remained relatively constant. This meant that they were still making the same cash profit from the sales they were achieving however the value of the stock on shelf more than doubled.

The figures contained in the table below are fictitious:

Note	Description	Before	After
1	Passengers	60,000	60,000
2	Monthly Sales ($)	288,000	288,900
3	Number of Transactions	7,200	3,210
4	Average Transaction Value ($)	40	90
5	Conversion	12.0%	5.4%
6	Spend Per Pax ($)	4.80	4.82

7	Average Units Per Transaction	2	1
8	Average Price Point ($)	20.00	90.00
9	Gross Margin ($)	50%	50%
10	Cash Margin ($)	144,000	144,450
11	Cost Value of Product Sold ($)	144,000	144,450
12	Units Sold	14,400	3,210
13	Average Cost Price Per Unit ($)	10.00	45.00
14	Days Cover	5	15.7
15	Units on Shelf	2,323	1,626
16	Stock Value ($)	23,230	73,170
17	Gross Margin Return on Inventory Investment ($)	6.20	1.97
18	Expected Annual GMROII ($)	74.40	23.69
19	Space (Ft)	1,000	1,000
20	Monthly Space Productivity $/Ft	288	289

So, let's take a look at the table above and break down the logic.

Note 1:

This represents the number of passengers that have gone through the airport. For simplicity, we will assume that the traffic is constant at 60,000 passengers in a month.

Note 2:

We stated that the sales have remained constant despite the change. Here we see a very slight increase in sales by $900 to $288,000.

Note 3:

We can see here that the number of transactions has fallen significantly from 7,200 in a month to 3,210.

Note 4:

Based on this finding, we can then calculate the Average Transaction Value (Total Sales divided by the number of transactions). In the new premiumised store, we see that the average transaction value has increased from $40 to $90. This is a significant increase.

Note 5:

As we have the number of transactions, we can also work out the conversion rate (Total Transactions divided by the Number of Passengers). This shows that before the change, the store converted 12% of pax. Since the change, the store now converts 5.4% of pax.

OK. We can see that the store has premiumised, it is converting less passengers into buyers but, when they do buy, they are buying more expensive items. This means that the store sales value remains constant but it needs to do less work in order to match the sales.

Note 6:

As a quick reference check, we can see that Spend Per Pax (Total Sales divided by the number of passengers) is relatively constant at $4.82.

Let's dig into the detail of the average transaction:

Note 7 & 8:

Here we see that on average, the number of items in the basket is 2 before the store change. Since the change, the average number of items in the basket is 1. From this, we can calculate the average price paid and we can see that the shopper is trading up but is going on to buy less items.

So what are the margin implications? Let's take a look:

Note 9:

An assumption has been made that he Margin % remains constant. This is 50%.

Note 10 & 11:

With this information, the Cost Value of the Good Sold and the Cash Margin figure can be calculated.

Note 12 & 13:

Because we know the number of units sold (Average Items per Transaction multiplied by the number of transaction), we can get a view on the average cost price per item.

Note 14 & 15:

Here we need to make an assumption on the level of days stock cover that is held in the store BEFORE the store changes. Days cover gives us a view on how many days the store can trade before it runs out of stock. Let us assume that the number of days stock cover is 5 days. If we know that the store sold 14,400 units in a month, we can calculate the amount of stock that was in the store (14,400 divided by 31 days and multiply it by 5). This gives us a stock holding of 2,323 on shelf. From here, we make another assumption – because the store has premiumised, let us assume that there is 30% less unit stock in the store. We take the 2,323 figure and multiply that by 0.7 to get 1,626 units in store. Now that we have a realistic assumption on the level of stock in store, we can calculate the value of that stock.

Note 16:

Multiply the stock holding in store by the average cost price per unit. This gives you $23,230 (2,323 x $10) of stock prior to the store change and $73,170 (1,626 x $45) of stock held in store after the change. Stock value held in store has more than tripled.

Note 17:

Now, let's get bring this all together:

- The store sales have remained flat
- The store is converting less passengers but they are spending more in each transaction
- The range has been changed to give it a more premium feel which requires higher value items in the store
- Cash margin has remained constant
- The store is effectively selling more for less 'work'

So what do the numbers say? Before the store changed, the Cash Margin generated for the month was $144,000. Divide this figure by the average stock sat on shelf ($23,230) and you get a Gross Margin Return on Inventory Investment of $6.20.

By comparison, after the store changed, the Cash Margin generated was $144,450 but the stock holding was $73,170. Once again, divide the Cash Margin by the average stock on shelf and you get a Gross Margin Return On Inventory Investment of $1.97.

It has taken more stock in terms of Cash Value to generate the same amount of Cash Margin.

Note 18:

It would be reasonable to assume for the purposes of this exercise that if we multiply the GMROII figure by 12, this will give us an annual forecast as follows:

| Before: | Annual GMROII = $74.39 |
| After: | Annual GMROII = $23.69 |

What this is saying is that for every $1 of stock held, the store is generating $74.39 in cash margin before the change and $23.69 of Cash Margin after the change.

Note 19 & 20:

Bringing it back to space – if we make the assumption too that the space remains unchanged at 1,000 feet of shelf space, the productivity remains unchanged. Total Sales divided by Shelf Space.

When you review this example, would you say that the store change is actually a good idea? This new concept store is now achieving the same level of sales as before, same profit as before but is now sitting on more than double the stock in cash terms. Good decision?

Let me put this into another context. I offer you a bank account. If you deposit $10,000 with me, I will give you $1,000 interest. Sounds like a great deal! A year later, I offer you a new deal. Deposit $30,000 with me and I will offer you $1,000 in interest. Still a great deal? Maybe not so much.

The concept we have discussed here is Gross Margin Return on Inventory Investment. This evaluates the return the retailer is getting on their stock investment. The retailer has now put themselves in a position where they are holding high value stock which is slow moving.

Has the retailer made a mistake? Is the premiumisation strategy a mistake?

Unfortunately, this cannot be answered in this example. The key to retail success is to anticipate the shoppers needs and wants and make sure that you have it there for when they arrive. The super-premium lines are appealing to a very different customer segment.

The shopper who is in the market for buying a $5,000 Cognac will not choose to buy a $100 Cognac if the $5,000 one is not available.

Summary

Within the Space Planning section we have considered:

- Why it is important to understand space
- How to measure and capture it
- Space productivity reporting
- Optimising space

We have also considered the challenges that a Space Planning department faces and how to overcome some of those challenges. We have also seen that Space Planning does not have to be the domain of just the retailer, brands can be involved too.

If you are a brand without a space planning function to support the retailer you can still:

- Spend time watching shoppers
  - Identify shopper flow and behaviour
  - See how fixtures, promotions and activations influence behaviour
  - See how the layout impacts staff behaviour
- Capture space for your category and brands
- Capture competitor brands space
- Evaluate your own space productivity
- Prepare to make recommendations and present them to the retailer

PART 8

THE TRAVEL RETAILER OF THE FUTURE

There are 3 key elements that will greatly influence the success of the Travel Retailer of the future. These are:

- The beliefs that it holds
- The ability to deal with adversity and instability
- The ability to continue to strive for excellence

The retailer that can question inherited beliefs from internal sources or from the industry and reframe them, will have the freedom to transform the quickest.

As we have seen, the Travel Retail market is a challenging place and the ability to be resourceful and adaptable leads to survival and success.

When you walk into a store you can tell immediately if it settles for mediocre. The stores that are striving for excellence stand out in the crowd. In these stores, the teams operate at their best, all day every day. There are no shortcuts to success.

Let's start with Beliefs....

Beliefs In Travel Retail

Travel Retail has some core fundamental beliefs that it has held close for decades. I want to challenge those beliefs in the hope that it will help propel the industry that we all know and love into the next era.

Those beliefs are as follows:

- Travel Retail delivers world class service
- Travel Retail has the best stores in the world
- Travel Retail offers great value for money
- Everyone wants what we have on sale.

These are beliefs that are rarely challenged and therefore are inhibiting the channel and slowing down its evolution. Do we REALLY offer world class service? Compared to what? Are our stores the really the best in the world? Maybe. Do we really offer great value? Probably not. Everyone certainly doesn't want what we offer but that is ok.

At World Duty Free I challenged these beliefs and I was labelled a 'Maverick' for that attitude and approach. No – I am not a brilliant Top Gun pilot, I just wanted every day to be better than the day before. I wanted to be on the frontiers, pushing our understanding, learning and perfecting our craft.

So how do we change these beliefs?

The simplest answer is to be able to focus on never ending continuous improvement, challenging what we believe to be true and having drive to move things forward.

It would be far better to adapt those beliefs to the following:

- Travel Retail is developing the best service experience in the world

- Travel Retail is striving to have the very best stores in the world
- Travel Retail enables shoppers to buy their favourite brands when they travel
- Travel Retail seeks to appeal to the broadest customer base

This version of the beliefs feels like it is more of a journey rather than a destination. It implies that we are forever moving forward and not resting.

I believe that this can be done by taking advantage of 3 key opportunities:

1. Operational Efficiency & Effectiveness
2. Become A Research Business That Sells Products
3. Enhancing Shopper Experience

The Ability To Deal With Adversity & Instability

The world is changing at an ever-increasing pace. Change can be positive but it can also be unnerving. The lack of perceived control can have a debilitating effect. Events such as pandemics, the ash cloud and even terrorism are all things that are beyond our control We must always seek to adapt to them. There are strategies that you can follow to help you cope with radical change and uncertainty.

In the chart below, you can see that there are 3 levels of control:

1. Things you can control
2. Things you can influence (but have no control over)
3. Things beyond your control and influence.

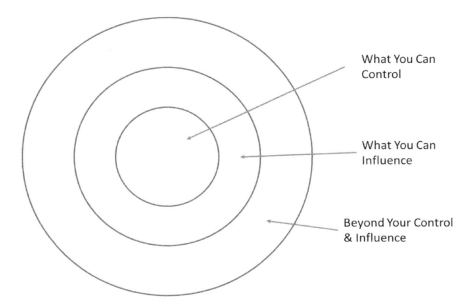

What You Can Control

What You Can Influence

Beyond Your Control & Influence

Whilst there are many things that are outside our control or influence, there is so much that we can prepare for to ensure our businesses remain agile in the toughest of situations.

As ever, there are other fields that we can learn from and this is no different. The time, lessons from the military environment...

VUCA

After the cold war, the US Army War College developed a concept called VUCA to describe the global situation. VUCA stands for Volatile, Uncertainty, Complexity and Ambiguity. Classifying unpredictable events in this way helps speed up make the decision-making process and navigate these situations more effectively.

- Volatility – relates to the pace of change
- Uncertainty – relates to the ability to predict the future
- Complexity – relates the number of moving parts within a specific problem
- Ambiguity – relates to the lack of clarity or information about a problem

VUCA doesn't have to be negative. It can bring positive challenge too. For example, companies such as Brew Dog and Fever Tree have seen massive expansion in a very short space of time. This rapid expansion would have brought with it Volatility, Uncertainty, Complexity and Ambiguity.

To overcome VUCA situations you can take actions, for example:

- Volatility – Build in some flexibility through additional resource
- Uncertainty – Undertake an information gathering exercise
- Complexity – Seek out to simplify processes and operations
- Ambiguity – Aim to test hypotheses to improve understanding

The key is not to freeze and become indecisive. "Progress, Not Perfection" (one of my favourite quotes from the film The Equalizer) has become the "ordre du jour".

Working in a global environment like Travel Retail, key stakeholders will invariably be dealing with VUCA situations.

Covid was the perfect example of a VUCA situation. Globally, governments were taking different approaches and actions to overcome the challenge of a pandemic. For air travel, advice was ever changing (Volatility), different parts of the world were coming back online at different times (Uncertainty), additional processes and procedures had to be taken into account to prevent the spread of the virus (Complexity) and no one could really predict how people would respond when they were able to travel (Ambiguity).

Covid therefore, ticked every box!

Some in our industry predicted that as an industry we may never recover. At One Red Kite, we believed in different. We were absolutely confident that the return would happen and happen, it did. We were also vocal about the need to 'prepare for the return'. As a business we used any available spare time to improve on what we do. Brands and Retailers should certainly do a post covid review to create a blueprint for what should be done if something like Covid happens again.

In reality, who knew that planes worldwide would ever be grounded? It is unimaginable.

The quirk that Travel Retail has is that despite how dynamic the travel market is, change is often resisted. That resistance I believe comes from a degree of emotion and sensitivity. Having worked in a dynamic, fast paced domestic retailer, I initially struggled with the pace that Travel Retail works at. In domestic, there was no time to be sensitive about things, it just had to be done. This meant decisions could be taken, action was taken and the business moved forward. Within Travel Retail, everything takes far longer than you would ever expect. In domestic, a decision could be made on a Monday morning and by Friday afternoon it was implemented in over 300 stores across the country.

As an industry, we need to be moving faster and to move faster, it needs to challenge some of those long-held beliefs.

So with beliefs that need to be revisited and a market that is certainly considered to be VUCA, what can Travel Retailers do to ensure continued resilience and success?

Introducing The Diamond Model

What is the Diamond Model?

The diamond model requires a very different approach and mentality. It is a process of re-engineering retail to be ready for the new era, the "new normal".

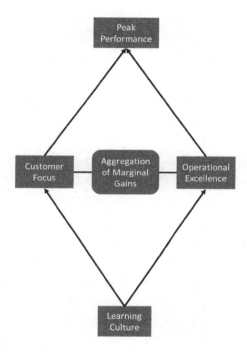

The Learning Culture

In the diagram above, we start at the bottom. To be relevant in the future, we need to refocus on becoming learning organisations. There is enormous value to be gained by taking a step back and taking a fresh look at how things are done. Every day, in every business there are opportunities to learn new and find better ways of doing things. If the customer is evolving, surely there are also new things to learn about the customer too.

It doesn't matter if you are retailer, an operator or a brand, learning more about your customers or shoppers can deliver the insights you need to create a competitive advantage.

There are 3 ways that Travel Retail can become a learning culture:

- Retailers should create their own in-house Market Research Agency. This would:
    - Drive incremental revenues
    - Accelerate the understanding of shoppers in any given location
    - Increase global collaboration and understanding
    - Give brands the real insight they need to best serve the market
- Brands should consider bringing local market knowledge to airports to help better understand the core audiences. Retailer data and research combined with local knowledge is a powerful combination
- Experiment & measure – Encourage the whole team to focus on testing and measuring the impact of every activity that has been implemented to grow sales. Ran a promotion? Measure it. Ran an activation? Measure it. Moved a subcategory to a new location? Measure it. Employed brand ambassadors? Measure it. This can then create a knowledge bank to help shape future strategies and actions.

This is a huge cultural shift for any organisation. It requires a clear understanding that failing is ok, as long as it has been a learning exercise.

The next part of the diamond is to utilise the learnings to:

- Focus on the shopper
- Deliver Operational Excellence

First, let's focus on the customer...

Customer Focus

For Travel Retail to succeed in the future, we must become obsessive about the customer. We have completed many Mystery Shopping studies over the years and whilst on the whole, the level of service is good, there is and always will be an opportunity to improve.

To drive customer focus, there are a number of ways that we can deliver better for our customers:

- Creating a better customer experience in store. The attention to detail and drive from the sales floor management team must be present all the time.
- Shopper Targeting can be taken to the next level. Retailers can utilise basket data to drive unparalleled insights. Combine this with the in-house market research agency and you will really be running on rocket fuel.
- Dynamic Retail Spaces is a concept I wrote about a few years ago and has recently been implemented in part in Europe. This is about assigning space within a store to test new concepts. Successful concepts can go on to become a permanent part of the store. This isn't about pop-ups which are usually an extension of existing categories. This is space to test new concepts.

Operational Excellence

Back in 1993, a fast Formula 1 Pit Stop would take 4.8 seconds to complete. If you could take a time machine back to 1993 and tell them that in 2019, a team would take 1.82 seconds to complete a pit stop, they would probably consider it to be impossible. However, a 1.82 second pit stop is exactly what was achieved in Brazil in 2019 by the Red Bull team.

The overall steps that happen during a pit stop are still fundamentally the same. The difference is that they have taken the finest details and sought to improve them. This has led to such a significant reduction in time spent out of action. They have refined what they do, changed the tools and have focused on doing the basics brilliantly. By having the relentless pursuit of excellence, they have taken almost 3 seconds off what would be considered to be a fast time.

When we consider Travel Retail, it has remained largely the same over the last couple of decades. Just like the Formula 1 Pit Crew, the time has come to review things with fresh eyes and see what can be changed.

An example of this is the work we have been doing with one of our clients. They had someone spending 1 day a week building their reports to deliver insights to the board. We took over the reporting responsibility. Now, they can access useful and practical insights in just a few clicks.

This has saved our client 1 day a week. It doesn't sound like much but that is 52 days per year, which is more than 10 working weeks! That individual now spends their time making decisions rather than wasting time building reports.

Every business, whether you are a brand, a retailer, an operator or another type of business working within Travel Retail, has the opportunity to find smarter ways of doing things.

Another way of creating operational excellence on the shop floor is to use the Discovery approach to selling. The Discovery approach uses a pre-defined set of questions in a particular order to get a shopper to close the sale quickly and easily. This method has been tried and tested in the domestic market and it delivers incredible results. The beauty of the discovery approach is that it enables flexibility to adapt the conversation in the way the customer wants to be served but also enables the salesperson to use a framework that can be followed.

Aggregation of Marginal Gains

This concept lies at the very heart of everything that the diamond model stands for. The concept of Aggregation of Marginal Gains was first used by Sir Dave Brailsford who was the head coach at the British Cycling Team and Team Sky. The principles of Marginal Gains are as follows:

- Break down every task into sub tasks (its smallest constituent parts)
- Compare the current performance of each subtask to a benchmark of optimum performance where possible
- Look to improve every subtask by at least 1%
- The cumulation of all the improvements of the subtasks lead to significant gains

In a documentary, Sir Dave Brailsford highlights the Team Sky Tour de France performance. They decided to use the Marginal Gains principles and set themselves a target of having a British rider winning the Tour de France within 5 years. It had never been done previously. After applying the principles and adapting their team culture, they won 2 in 4 years. This is an outstanding achievement, one that was possible thanks to focusing on doing things better, even if it were only a little better.

So how does this approach apply to Travel Retail. Regardless of your business, the concept of Marginal Gains applies. It is a concept that we have been using within One Red Kite for some time. We look back on what we did a year ago and we can see a real step change in performance. We did things really well last year and delighted our customers. Now our processes are even better, smarter and more robust. We could have settled with what we were doing but we have that drive to always be improving.

Another example of where we have helped a client is to enable them to automate their rebate calculations. This means that their Finance team can spend their time doing other things instead of manually building reports and running calculations. Once again, our support has delivered significant benefits.

One final example is from Domestic Retail. When I was working for Dixons Group, they optimised the shop floor team during peak season (10 weeks over Christmas and New Year). The drew on the Formula 1 pit crew analogy where the Salesperson was the driver and all other tasks surrounding the sale were handed over to other staff. The logic? Well, the salesperson who has been trained on products and how to sell them needs to be spending as much of their time selling. If someone comes in and buys a PC on credit, should that person be spending their time filling out a credit application? Or should that salesperson be back out on the shop floor selling? All the task around the sale was essentially taken away. The salesperson didn't have to process the transaction, they didn't have to go and get the item from the stock room, they didn't need to arrange any deliveries etc.

Everything was focused on that salesperson spending time talking to shoppers. Everything. It is the salesperson that has the necessary skillset to get people to buy and trade up. The best use of their time is selling.

Focusing on marginal gains really is about focusing on those minor details. It is about bothering with the smallest of things because that will lead to an enhanced experience for the shopper and better performances. It might be the position of the baskets in store, it might be the dust on shelves and products, it might even be that damn lightbulb that is out..... obsess about the detail!

The other thing to remember is that focusing on marginal gains is a lifestyle. There is no end to it. Take this book for example. I am sure there will be things in here that could be done better, but there has to be a point where you have to move forward. Remember, progress not perfection. Marginal gains is a driving force behind progress in search of perfection.

Binging It All Together – Peak Performance

When you consider everything, it really boils down to one simple word. Obsession.

You need the right people around you that believe in your vision and strive to deliver it. An organisation that believes it can and will be better will work towards that. An organisation that obsesses over the needs of the shopper and strives to be as efficient as possible to deliver that will ultimately succeed.

Can Peak Performance happen?

Absolutely. I have seen it happen time and time again because I have been part of teams that have obsessed and strived to deliver better. Obsession should not just come from the top down. It should come from the front line and up too. It is about people being passionate about success and helping each other succeed.

In short, the Diamond Model is about the following:

- Don't just do, study.
- Focus on developing brilliant basics
- Practice
- Be customer centric
- Obsess over marginal gains

Transform the way you do things to drive incremental growth for your business.

The Focus

The focus for Travel Retail over the next 5 years should centre around 3 streams.

1. Operational Efficiency & Effectiveness
2. Become A Research Business That Sells Products
3. Enhancing Shopper Experience

Whether you are a retailer, brand or even an operator, the things that underpin all aspects of this are as follows

- Squeezing every ounce of value out of your Data
- Developing effective reporting
- Undertaking detailed promotional evaluation
- Focus on simplicity
  - It is about selling product
  - Do the basics Brilliantly
  - Give them a reason to buy
  - Remove barriers to buying

When it comes to data, One Red Kite are specialists at turning data from different sources into something that is clean and easy to use. The team are trained to take a retailer perspective on the data and so they can add value. To us, it is never about churning files, care and attention goes into everything we do.

We are pioneers when it comes to working with data. We have developed and continue to refine our own industry specific software that creates new insights for our channel. Whether it is shopper targeting (a concept I developed while at WDF) or promotional evaluation, we have the capability to support your needs.

We even have the ability to convert your dark data into something useable. Dark data is the data you have locked away but are not using.

Connected to data is the possibility of creating a new revenue stream through research. We are already talking to retailers about how we can help them create their own revenue streams through enhanced shopper research. This would deliver powerful insights quickly and effectively for brands.

Finally, we also do Mystery Shopping.... But differently. We have never been identified in all the years we have been doing them. We do not do a tick box exercise. We focus on understanding your business, evaluating performance of your brands and competitor brands and give actionable insights. All our mystery shoppers are ex-retail managers who know exactly what should be happening in store, the strengths and weaknesses in store and how to drive performance.

PART 9

BETTER TRAVEL RETAIL

To summarise, to achieve Better Travel Retail, I believe we need to take the following steps.

1. Better Relationships
   a. Better dialogue through retailer terminology
   b. Focus on the shopper not market share
2. Change our reality
   a. Acknowledge that we are not for everyone. Yet.
   b. Instead of focusing on "why not", focus on the "how"
3. Focus on Service
   a. Exceed expectations
   b. Invest in the right things
   c. Invest in active selling skills
   d. Drive product knowledge
4. Utilise Basket Analysis
   a. Mine it, Package it, Sell it
   b. Optimise performance
   c. Better targeting
   d. Better research
   e. voyager
5. Use Space Planning as a Catalyst
   a. The small cog that aligns everything

b. Tighter controls over range

c. Evaluate, Evaluate, Evaluate

6. Change how we market the channel

a. Better Strategy

b. Better Targeting

c. Better Positioning

7. Try the Diamond Model

8. Create a sense of urgency

Relationships – Retailers & Brands

One topic that invariably comes up in meetings is the challenge of relationships between retailers and brands. Both sides will often say that the other party is failing to listen but having sat 'both sides of the fence' I often see that there is far more common ground than either party realise. There is a relatively simple fix to this and one that we have proved can work.

At One Red Kite we run a 2-day course for brands on how to better understand the retailer. Attendees leave the course with a clearer understanding of why retailers do some of the things that they do and how to approach them differently to improve dialogue and relationships. For those who have worked in Travel Retail will know that it is a relationship business and therefore a people business.

In one situation, a brand really wanted to help a retailer to grow their sales but needed data. The retailer was very restrictive on how much data it released to the brand – in fact, you could fit the numbers they released on a business card! We helped them turn those numbers into a story to show that the retailer was heading for a problem. We coached the Key Account Manager on how best to talk through the findings and they went to see the retailer. This simple approach unlocked the data they needed to help the retailer transform their performances. How can one conversation create such a significant change? Here are some of the reasons below. You might be doing some of these or maybe all of these already. It is worth revisiting again and seeing if there is a new perspective.

Influencing The Retailer

Speak Their Language

I have worked for a retailer and I have worked with brands. The one thing that I have noticed is that although a brand and a retailer will often be talking about the same topics, there is a lack of mutual understanding. I quickly realised that brands speak a different 'language' to the retailer. In one situation I was attending a meeting with a brand. The meeting wasn't moving forward in the way that the brand had hoped and the body language of those attending from the retailers side was clearly defensive, unengaged and dismissive. When a suitable opportunity arose, I started to talk about the merits of the brands suggestions but in a very subtly different way. I had translated the message into retailer terminology. I talked about Spend Per Head, Passengers, Category, Metrics and more. Very quickly, the retailers body language changed. It was a like a lightbulb had gone on and they were thinking "ahh... you get it". The conversation changed very quickly and it achieved a positive outcome.

Brands can often get bogged down in their own terminology, their own language and their own way of seeing the world. Those working for brands can often believe that their product is the only worthwhile product and why would you even consider buying an alternative?? I have seen this go to an extreme level where a Key Account Manager would only buy their own brands in a bar. I asked them what they liked about the product and the response? "In truth, I hate the stuff but I have to be seen to be buying the brand". Wow.

Brands need to take a step out of their bubble and into the retailer's bubble. Become the retailer, see what they see, empathise with them, ask questions, understand their inner workings and the challenges they face. So few brands do this and so if you do, more often than not, they will welcome you with open arms.

Remember, Your Brand Is Not Special

It is easy to think that you have the best brands in the world but to a retailer, you are just one of many brands they deal with. Your products will appeal to a certain type of customer who is prepared to spend a certain amount for a product that they need. The customer might buy into your brands, your company ethos, your company values but.... Not everyone does.

The retailer needs to have an array of products to meet the wide-ranging needs of the shopper. Yes, you might have the biggest share of the category or you might give the best margin percentage (remember – "you can't eat percentage") or you might have the best activations. What you must remember is that there will be hundreds of other brands that the retailer needs to deal with, to negotiate with and to consider. Your voice is just one of many. This means that you need to differentiate yourself (not just your product) and build a relationship that creates value way beyond the cash margin from the sales generated from your products.

If you have a meeting with the buyers or marketing, your meeting may just be one of many that day. Making a good impression or getting the outcome you want takes more than just telling the retailer about your new products that are coming out. This section will help you.

Don't Steal

I cannot emphasise this enough. The aim of the retailers is to grow their business. For that to happen they either need to get more people to shop in their store or to get people to spend more when they buy. This will either be by trading up or putting more items into their basket.

Brands are often driven by market share but this is not ideal as the focus soon descends into attacking competitor brands. This is NOT what the retailer wants. If Brand A takes share from Brand B and Brand A's products are less profitable for the retailer, the retailer makes less money, even if sales remain constant.

For this reason, you must ALWAYS talk about growing the category (often referred to as growing the pie) because if the category grows and your share remains constant, you will benefit.

Your products should primarily be about luring new customers into the store, getting them to buy more or getting them to trade up – NOT about stealing share. One point to note – Retailers are not stupid. They will see through a flimsy pitch and spot a "me too" product a mile off (a "me too" product is one that has very similar features and benefits to a competitor product).

Another way of selling into a retailer is to tap into new markets to define a new category or take a niche category and expand it. Gin is a great example of how a tiny category has exploded and driven incremental sales. Remember when "World Foods" were a couple of bays in a supermarket? Or "Free From" or even Vegan?

Be Practical

Being practical and pragmatic is key. Whilst retailers love a bit of wow and pizazz and excitement, they are also very realistic about what can and cannot be done. The complications of getting fixtures to the right fire standards, health and safety, airside passes etc. can make things very difficult and time consuming. Anything that can save time and or work will be gratefully received. Remember – it is all about simplicity and value. Show that and you will begin opening so many doors.

Provide Solutions

Talk to retailers in terms of 'pre-packed solutions'. Show the retailer that you have thought through options and practicalities and that you can make recommendations that will deliver trouble free and stress free outcomes. Those working for retailers are busy people and anything that removes the need to think or extra work are what they will gravitate towards. Do as much as you can to take tasks away and remove obstacles and resistance.

Be Proactive

If you spot something, talk to them. If you receive your sales data and you have had a promotion on – be on the front foot and talk through an evaluation you have done. Promotional analysis is often something that the retailers do not get enough time to do.... So do it for them. Present your findings but in a way that shows that you still have questions. This encourages a dialogue.

Another way to be proactive is to offer to visit stores, capture photos and send a report. Always think about value beyond your product. What is it you can do to help them. If you go store and you see your section is a mess or being relaid – help the store and then send the buyer an update and a couple of photos. "I saw that the team were super busy helping customers so I rolled up my sleeves and helped them implement the planogram change. Looks great doesn't it (include a photo). I had lots of customers have questions about a certain type of product. Can we book in a call so I can share that feedback?". This will work wonders for building the relationship with the retailer.

Take Tasks Away

I remember talking to a buyer in domestic retail. He went on to say that he was prepared to give up margin percentage if a brand was willing to take some of his tasks away from him. Got a space planning department? Offer to create planograms. Have a team of analysts? Offer to support on analysis or do a range review for them? Have a field team. Offer to send images through to the retailer. I am sure you can think of lots of ways you can help the retailer by taking task away.

It is all too easy to think about "what is the minimum I can to do?" however, this doesn't build relationships or trust.

Offer to Evaluate

When you run a promotion, offer to evaluate it. This goes beyond what has been mentioned above in terms of being proactive. This goes a stage further by doing more. If you have captured research or shopper data during the promotion / activation, consider how that can be turned into something of value that the retailer can benefit from.

Another way of evaluating is to ask for the basket data for the transactions with your product in. This allows you to do a true evaluation of your activity to see how many people have bought the product on a multibuy for example and their passenger profile (destination, nationality, time of day etc).

Giving back rich insights will help you build a great relationship and better activations in the future. Prove the value you can deliver and you may be able to walk away with better margins.

Be Visible When It Matters

I cannot stress this enough. Being visible is absolutely key, particularly in busy times. An example of this is at Christmas. Many people working for brands go on holiday early December and return in January. The smart Key Account Managers go to key stores and work there. Retailers really appreciate this (Not all, but most). Going into a store on Christmas Eve might not seem appetising but it is a fantastic opportunity to speak to customers, gather anecdotal insights from shoppers, build connections with the front line and sell more of your product! Such an action is seen in a very positive light by the retailers. It shows you are committed to them and their category.

One piece of advice though... DO remember to "think category" and sell your competitors products too. Flip it round so that YOU are achieving value. Ask the buyer why they are choosing your competitors product. This gives you some useful insight to help you think about positioning your brand and products in the eyes of the customer, retailer and competitors.

Remember, they know their business!

Another key point to remember. As a brand, you know your brand. A retailer knows their category and their business. They have a greater understanding of the big picture and what is happening, respect that. If they disagree with your views and opinions, it is worth noting that they have access to more knowledge than you do. This may be in terms of margin percentage, supply, growth patterns, passenger profiles and shifting flight schedules etc. Instead of thinking "they are wrong", ask them why they take a particular position on something. It will pay dividends in the long run. The more you can glean, the better you will understand them and how they think... the better you can influence them.

Drop The Arrogance

It is all too easy to go into a retailer thinking that you are the answer to all their prayers. You have the best brands right? That may be so. Manners and a little patience cost nothing but go a very long way with a retailer. Don't be pushy or demanding. Be respectful, listen and watch those doors open to a world of opportunities.

Influencing The Front Line

Remembering the front line

There have been many times when I have been chatting to people who work within brands and asked them "When was the last time you went into store?". The responses vary from "When I have to for travel" through to "Never". Those that have responded as "Never" are those that travel but avoid going into store. This for me is a massive, missed opportunity. There is so much value to either going into store or being stood outside it.

Firstly, if you are not prepared to visit the store, why should your customers? The people who buy your product! Secondly, the people who are often the face of your brand (because they are actually selling it) are there. Isn't it a good idea to make contact? Ask them questions? Talk about your brand? Get their buy in? Engage with them? These are the people that can have an influence over whether a shopper buys your product or your competitor product.

Staff in store love a bit of TLC (tender loving care). Show interest in them, nurture them and you will have them selling your product through choice rather than just as part of an incentive.

Word does get back to buyers when brand have been in and made a good impression.

Getting managers on-board

It is always useful to get the in-store managers onboard and engaged with your brand. They need to be made to feel important (because they are) and so it is good to talk to them, get their thoughts. Help them help you understand what is going on the front lines. There will be opportunities for you and your company to get involved and help them. Do they need some training? Do they need some support for a store relay? Do they need salespeople to cover them while they do a training day? In retail, there is always something to be done and something you can help them with.

Target the salespeople - make a connection

When you are talking to those on the front line, find those special stars who are masters of selling to shoppers. Sit outside a store for a while and watch to see which ones are highly motived to sell. You can often find them. They are usually the ones that either avoid sales floor chat or if they are talking, they are scanning the shop floor looking for opportunities. The best have 2 or maybe 3 shoppers on the go and selling all of them. They are confident enough to leave a customer while they move on to the next. Watching them is like watching someone spin plates. These are the people to target.

For some, retail is a real vocation. They love the thrill of the chase and will go all out to smash targets even if there is no incentive or commission. They are driven. I have seen some people who outperform the average sales by a multiple of 3 on a typical day. That means they account for 3 times the sales that the average salesperson achieves.

So why target these people? Well... if they are doing that much volume and throughput – the chances are they are going to be the best people to engage. Get them onboard with your brands and encourage them to sell more of your product. You will need to give them a reason to sell your products over a competitors. Take some time to learn about what they do well, how they do it and why. What is it that motivates them?

To smash YOUR targets, you are going to want highly motivated people to be selling your product. Engage with them.

Training

Salespeople can only go so far without product knowledge. If they do not know about your product, they cannot sell it in the way you intended. There is so much that a salesperson can be talking about including heritage (where your brand comes from), brand stories (particularly prevalent in Whisky), the features of the products or flavour profile, the benefits and why your product is priced the way it is.

Another factor to consider – do the salespeople have the skills to actually sell your products? Or any products for that matter? Are they people who are there to earn money to buy beer at the weekend or do they see their job as something they love and enjoy?

This is another situation where it is important to engage those with potential. This means targeting those that 'could' become the next sales stars. These are the people with a bit of energy, flair and empathy but do not necessarily have the right sales skills to ask open questions, match products to their needs and close the sale. The plan should be to encourage the next wave of sales superstars. You might wonder why this should be any concern to a brand as surely it is the responsibility of the retailer to train their teams. You might be right in thinking that but if it makes the difference between smashing your targets, better relationships with the front line and the buyers or missing it.... What would you do? Exactly. Go beyond selling boxes / product and really engage with those that talk with shoppers every day.

Product Knowledge

I am going to re-emphasise this again. Product knowledge is key. It is so frustrating as a shopper to be dealing with someone who lacks confidence in the knowledge they have on a product or brand. Getting the salesperson trained up on some simple facts is critical.

When training people about your brand and products it is one thing to tell them about your brand, it is another to package it up in a way that is memorable. Using stories, mnemonics, sounds and imagery are all keys to successful knowledge sharing. The most important thing is not to overload the recipient with facts and statistics. They won't remember it. It is worth noting that they will have lots of brands to think about when they are selling. Something as simple as – can you see the bear in the Toblerone logo? Is enough of a fascinating fact to help the salesperson to open a conversation or remember some pertinent facts.

You do need to be careful when training, however. One mystery shop in the Whisky category led to a sales assistant telling one of our mystery shoppers that a particular brand of Whisky had a fishy smell. Maybe not the most appetising way of selling a product.

Be Present / visible

I am going to emphasise this point too. Even when you are flying through an airport on business (or even a holiday) and you really do not have time – at least make yourself known to someone on the shop floor. Ideally say hello to a store / duty manager. A few minutes of your day can make a significant impact on theirs. Of course, it also enables you to find out a few facts on how the store is trading which will help with your conversations in head office.

Sales Driven Managers

A little more of a long-term perspective here but developing store and duty managers is a soft power approach to enhancing performance in stores. Engaging them, training them indirectly and getting them onboard with your approach and perspective can have a significant impact. This works particularly well where a retailer does not have processes in place like space planning, range control, a comprehensive sales training program etc. A culture can be influenced from the front line and can shape the landscape of the store.

This might be considered as crossing a few boundaries for some and a little bit too forward. However, I would argue that as long as you are doing it for the good of the store /

category, the retailer will win and in turn, so will you, the brand.

Summary

As I mentioned at the start of this section, the relationships between the retailers and the brands can often be challenging but this does not need be the case. There have been so many times I have seen a retailer and brand essentially saying the same thing but because the 'language' is different, relationships are not as productive as they could be. My advice if you are a brand is to do the following:

- Think like a retailer
- Speak like a retailer
- Act like a retailer

Really engage with the retailer, understand them and learn what is important to THEM. Once you have cracked that, you will know how to best position your brand and product to get the outcomes you want and need faster and more effectively.

In simple terms:

- **Stop** – Put your agenda on hold
- **Listen** – Really listen to what the retailer is saying
- **Understand** – Check that you understand their situation completely
- **Align** – Think about how you can align your needs with theirs
- **Suggest** – Show the retailer how your solutions will help solve their challenges

Change Our Reality

The world has changed over the last 30 years. It has probably changed more in the last 2 years than in the last 20. It is time to recognise that and change some of the fundamental beliefs that we have about our industry. It is time to challenge and question and come up with a new reality, one that is realistic and will drive growth and change.

Change is always difficult, even when it seems like the easiest choice with the greatest rewards but change we must. It is one of life's inevitabilities.

So where do we start? Let's shatter some myths....

Everyone Wants What We Have

Travel Retail can often be wrapped up in its own bubble with a belief that the everyone wants what is available in Duty Free stores. The view "well why *WOULDN'T* you buy in the Duty Free Airport" is a view that needs be dropped.

Let's face fact. Not everyone wants what we sell..... and that is never going to change. For example, if someone is against drinking alcohol, it is unlikely that they will ever buy from the Liquor department, even for a gift. If someone doesn't believe in having a skin care routine and having one has never even occurred to them, you are unlikely to get them into the store to see, try and buy.

I remember going to a conference years ago and there was a guest speaker. It came across like it was beyond his understanding as to why someone wouldn't spend £500 on a tie. Considering the vast majority of the audience wouldn't have that level of disposable income, it was one speech that some might consider to be a little 'tone deaf'.

We need to stop making the assumption that every single person flying through the airport loves and wants what we have. As soon as we recognise that, we can move forward, adapt our message and become stronger. We need to appeal to a wider target audience by appealing to them with different categories and products.

Instead Of Focusing On The "Why Not", Focus On The "How"

Over the years there has been much discussion about why people are not buying the core categories. In today's retail, we need to think about how we can either influence people to buy into the core categories or think about other categories that people might also be interested in.

Focusing on the "Why are people not buying?" places emphasis on the objections and not on the solutions. If the shopper says the price is too high – well.... What are you going to do about that when there are others that are prepared to pay the prices in store? If someone says that they didn't have the brand they were looking for – so which brands do they want? (This is a question that is never answered in the research I have seen. It is also a polite way for people to say something they think the researcher wants to hear). If they say that they were just killing time..... ok, how does a store overcome that? This focus is all on the limits in the hope that we will find a gem of insight that will transform the channel.

Bottom line is, I am not seeing anyone ask, how are we going to attract a new audience into the stores. A new audience is likely to come from category extension or new categories.

Prices Keep Rising & People Will Keep Paying

The push to premiumise continues, however more and more shoppers are going to start to feel excluded. Value is there for those who have high levels of disposable income. For those who have less disposable income available to them, there are less options for them to spend money. In some locations, even a bottle of water has become very expensive.

At the time of writing (2022) the prospect of a hard recession is looming. Unemployment is likely to rise, cost of living is rising due to inflation and travel itself may become more of a luxury.

Airport retail will soon reach a point where it becomes no longer worthwhile spending. The savings that offset the inconvenience of carrying product onboard with you are barely there anymore.

In short, shoppers are smarter than we give them credit for and they will shift their spend into other areas.

Focus On Service

Unfortunately, in today's retail world, service is seen as a cost. Stripping out head count does indeed save money but then again, I have seen the power of active selling first-hand. The trend seems to be moving towards a "self-service" style of retail with digital replacing people. The exception here is Beauty, of course, but even that is changing at the moment.

Travel Retail is a unique environment and there is a fantastic opportunity to create something special for shoppers. That point of difference is people. So what can we do to win in Travel Retail?

Exceed Expectations

Ever heard that phrase – Always under promise and over deliver? Well... it is sound advice and for good reason. It is a simple reminder to manage expectations effectively. People judge services, products, people... Just about anything based on what their preconceived ideas are telling them. You might believe in telling shoppers about your exceptional service levels but you might be surprised to know that this is counter intuitive. Telling people that you offer an exceptional level of service primes the shopper to expect the very best service and of course, service is subjective. What one person might feel is superb, another might consider to be substandard and poor. This creates a dilemma.

Should you position yourself to have exceptional service or do you emphasise another quality but internally as a business you strive for the ultimate levels of service? To give you an example – In the UK there is a famous department store that positions itself to have exceptional service at low prices. This sets up high expectations in the shoppers mind. They might even have images of the red carpet being rolled out for them!

The problem is the service levels they actually deliver are average at best. The price promise feels like they hope you don't check and the merchandising, although at a first impression looks great, is confusing and frustrating. You often walk out feeling deflated and frustrated. What does that say about the company and the brand? Your high expectations have not been met.

On the flip side, stores such as Aldi (for me anyway) carry the perception of low service standards and that is how they can manage to sell products at cheaper prices. However, stop and ask someone working on the shop floor for some help and I have always received incredible service from a polite and helpful member of staff.

The key then is to make customer service your focus.... But not shout about it to customers. Surprise and delight them in a friendly, helpful and polite way to ensure that their expectations have been exceeded.

This approach works well between brands and retailers. Brands should always try to go the extra mile for the retailer, do something that isn't expected and it will be appreciated.

Now, please do not go around setting very low expectations in order to massively exceed them. It will work against you. You must be clear on what you are promising in terms of service and it must be perceived as adequate – not below or above adequate. It should be adequate.

In short, if you set out to exceed expectations, you will be heading in the right direction in terms of service.

Invest In The Right Things

Service is such a broad subject and it is important to understand what matters most to your customers. There are a variety of surveys that retailers can use to identify this. Parasuaraman et al group these into 5 key elements including:

- Reliability – Does the retailer always do what they say they will?
- Assurance – How confident does the customer feel during and after the service has been provided?
- Tangibles – How does the store show up in terms of quality of fixtures, ticketing etc?
- Empathy – Does the customer feel like they have been listened to?
- Responsiveness – How quickly did the service provider respond

There may be several elements to each of these 5 areas.

The key is to measure customer expectations and compare that to perceptions. These authors refer to it as the SERVQUAL methodology.

So, for example, if a retailer puts massive efforts into delivering a very high standard for its fixtures, ticketing, uniforms etc but these things are not important for the shopper (as in the chart below – see

A), it is likely to be a waste of resources. The retailer is over delivering vs expectations.

Service Standards

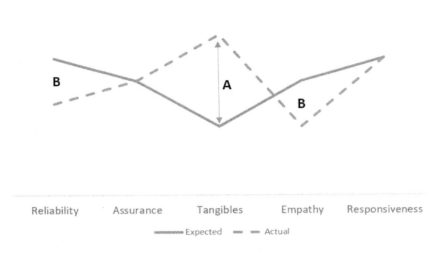

| Reliability | Assurance | Tangibles | Empathy | Responsiveness |

Expected ━━ ━━ Actual

However, in this scenario, there are situations where the retailer is underperforming (see **B** in the chart above). Reliability is the most important factor and they are missing the mark. Empathy is also something that the retailer is underperforming on.

This means that the retailer is potentially investing in the wrong things. They are focusing on beautiful stores but they fall short on delivering on their promises and making the customer feel like they are understood. A small, cost effective change could make all the difference to the shopper experience and therefore deliver significant benefits.

It is important that brands and retailers invest in the right elements of service to ensure that passengers, shoppers and buyers receive the right experience every time.

We have helped brands identify the biggest gaps in their service experience. We have enabled them to highlight what parts of their training works (based on how their brand ambassadors are operating on the shop floor), what doesn't work as well as what they need to adjust. Brands will often deliver training thinking that they have put the right amount of emphasis on Heritage or Product Knowledge but in reality, they have missed the mark. This means that the trainers can cost effectively *adapt* their training (not throw everything out and start again) and refine it until it delivers the right outcome they need.

Invest in Active Selling Skills

During our bespoke mystery shopping trips the biggest failing we see in store is the inability to sell. Even when you are putting out strong buying signals (just short of a neon sign above your head), these are either ignored or not recognised by staff. This means that potential buyers are walking away without buying something and the money is not in the till. Those that DO buy are the ones that have strong intent to buy. As mentioned previously, staff in store might just go for the "low hanging fruit" and trade people down. We need to focus on turning bodies on the shop floor into super sales people who can convert browsers into buyers and get them spending more than they had considered spending.

When I see a plane in the sky, I see cash that could have been in the till. If you as a retailer or brand want to win in Travel Retail, you need to create a level of hunger and the skill set to satisfy that hunger.

Drive Product Knowledge

The basics of retail are pretty simple. If you want to sell something in a store it needs to be:

- In stock with adequate quantity
- On shelf (NOT in the warehouse)
- Visible & faced up (meaning that it is brought to the front of the shelf)
- Clean

- Ticketed
- Sellable

Now, all of the above are pretty straightforward to understand although it might surprise you that in some retailers you may find product still sat out in the stock room and not on shelf. The one that might make you look twice is the "sellable". Surely if you have done all of the above, being "sellable" is something that should be automatic?

When I refer to something being sellable, I mean that the Features, Advantages & Benefits must be clear. This might be a little difficult for some retailers where information is not on the ticket and this is where product knowledge is key.

To re-emphasise the points already made about product knowledge and training, if you can, get out into your key stores as often as you can. Speak to the staff, win hearts and minds and get them to a point where the product they know the most about is yours. Be creative and innovative. Incentivise and encourage people to learn more about your brand and to sell it. You might think your brand sells itself – it doesn't matter. You are not looking for share of shelf now, you are looking for share of mind. When a customer asks for a recommendation in your category, your brand should be the first thing they refer to.

Create a Sense of Urgency

Since arriving in Travel Retail in 2003, there has one thing that has never changed. The lack of urgency. I had come from a retail background where everything needed to be done yesterday. I would present my numbers at 8am on a Monday, decisions would be made in that meeting, the Point-of-Sale team would be briefed that morning, it would be signed off by Wednesday and be implemented on the Friday in over 330 stores. That... is speed.

Within Travel Retail, decisions can take FOREVER. I have never really understood why this might be the case? What is the reason for such caution? Why the indecision? Is it because we have a culture that is too consultative and engaging and so everyone needs to have a say and be involved?

I think back to a store re-lay I wanted to do back when I worked in Space Planning for World Duty Free. I had to create plans, options, rationale and justification. I had all the facts, analysis and business case to support the change. I then had to engage with key stakeholder to get buy in. I then had to take those key stakeholders out to the store to walk them through it. They discussed it between themselves and decided to leave the store as it was even though the option I was presenting was the right thing to do from a commercial perspective. Weeks of work had just gone down the drain.

So let's deconstruct this for a moment. It was a small outer store, the sales impact would have been negligible on both the store and the rest of the business. It was going to be a test case for significant stock reduction / efficiency. The plan I had created was to free up stock so that it could be sold in the main stores instead of gathering dust in an outer store. It would have made the return on stock investment much higher in that store, it would have made it simpler to shop and it would have delivered key learnings.

I remember watching everyone stood with the plans discussing it. For me, it made commercial sense, for them it was about protecting their categories. I did a quick calculation in my head and having all these people in the store was costing money. It should not have even been a debate. It should have just happened. The outcome would have been no loss in sales from less stock in the store. In fact, it was likely to have increased sales.

I was so frustrated. However, it wasn't just WDF. I have seen it everywhere and I think it is part of the fabric of Travel Retail. The thing that I find bemusing is that when decisions are finally made, there is very little follow up to see if those decisions have actually delivered against the forecast or plan. The Travel Retail bus just moves on.

Urgency is not one of Travel Retail's strong points. Decision making is often deferred or passed on and you end up with management by consensus which clogs up the mechanism and leads to paralysis.

I want to take a moment to reframe things.

Travel Retail is very lucky. It has a flow of traffic / passengers / shoppers that see the store once or twice a year. We have the ability to try things for short periods of time, measure them and make decisions. If we get something wrong, it is unlikely to echo into the coming weeks and months like it would in a supermarket with weekly shoppers.

In reality, when you start looking at sales from a Spend Per Head perspective and overlay activations and promotions you soon realise that it takes a lot to move the needle. If that is the case, the risks of doing some trials become very low indeed.

I remember another exercise where I wanted to change the layout in a main store. I fought hard for months. I had taken all of my learnings and observations during my time in stores, combined it with analysis and I knew it was the right thing to do with the existing passenger flow. My recommendation was continuously blocked. Eventually, the director gave in and the store layout was finally changed. The sales went up, the instore feedback was super positive and it was considered to be a success... Until a new part of the terminal opened a few weeks later and changed the passenger flow. The store had missed out on months of higher sales and a better shopper experience all because of the indecision from one individual. In that scenario, it should have just been done and if the layout didn't work, move it back a few weeks later. Of course, there are costs involved, a night crew coming into the store to move it around but I have seen cash wasted on other trivial projects. However, in this situation, the return on investment would have been significant.

The new layout was touted as a failure because of the change in passenger flow but I could prove that it was a successful layout in the right situation. I also knew that those in store thought it had worked too. Office politics got in the way.

I am reminded of a conversation that I had when I went into Dixons Head Office to work in the product marketing team. My manager welcomed me to the category and told me that she had high expectations and that poor performance would not be tolerated. I was a little concerned by this as some of my categories were declining (namely video tapes!). I asked her "if I am trying lots of things to grow sales and it isn't working, what then?". She replied, "if you are seen to be trying and seen to be doing something, that is ok. There are things that will be outside your control that you cannot do anything about. Work hard, do something and it will be noticed". This has never left me. It has been advice that I have carried forward with me and used to great effect.

I soon developed the belief that if you know a certain action is the right thing to do, every day you do not take action is a day wasted. So, if you believe that a change in store would lead to an extra £5,000 in sales per day, by the end of the week you have lost £35,000. This builds up until you implement that change. In some situations, in Travel Retail, I have seen changes take a year for a change to be made. In this scenario, that would have cost the business over £1.8m.

One way to speed up evolution is to create a test area in store. Set out some space that enables new categories and/or brands to be trialled and experimented with. This dynamic space can change according to season, passenger profile and it creates a new feature. It has the power to bring in new shoppers who currently simply walk past the store. Aldi are very good at doing this in their 'middle aisle'

– why can't Travel Retail do a luxury or premium version of this. It could be interesting. It might work, it might not... but you do not know until you try. If you find a category that works particularly well, introduce it permanently.

I am sure there will be some that grumble and challenge from our channel when reading this but I think it needs to be said. There is a growing voice from deep within the industry that concurs with this view – that we must bring a sense of urgency into the channel.

My advice – do things, experiment, try new approaches.... But measure it. Gather those learnings and store them; become a learning organisation. Doing nothing will not lead to gaining valuable knowledge, it will lead to stagnation. Be brave, try new things and see what happens. Situations like COVID do have their silver linings, they force companies to adapt and evolve in order to survive. It encourages decision making and faster responses to things.

That may just be it. Survival. In domestic retail, every day is a fight to survive. Narrow margins, tiny net profit percentages and an uphill struggle from all sorts of variables.... Including competition! Every single £ is fought for. Within the airport, it is a protective bubble that retailers can operate with relative comfort. Yes, retailers do still need to compete for their share of wallet but they do not have another retailer in the airport selling the same or remarkably similar products. The lack of direct competition can stifle innovation and prevent change.

You want to win in Travel Retail? Make some decisions, take action, act like you are on a burning platform every day. Drive the business hard and persist.

Test & Measure

I have mentioned this a number of times by now but I really cannot emphasise enough the benefits of Test and Measure. It really is the one thing that all retailers and brands should be doing to gain a deeper understanding of the actions they are taking. Quite often, I hear companies say that they do not have the resources to spend time on assessing how well or poorly the actions they have taken have done. This, I believe, is false economy.

One pushback I have also seen on this stance is from brands who say that they do not have data. When I ask them about the data they DO have, I usually find that there is enough there to uncover a story to tell the retailer and create a dialogue.

Brands often have an interesting perspective on data. The common situation is that the brands have Key Account Managers around the world that receive data from retailers in different formats. The Key Account Managers then have to extract that data themselves (which is time consuming) and then analyse it. The KAM's often do not have the time to do this as effectively as they could – after all, their job is to sell right? This means that the data they are using is often not accurate. This inaccurate data then gets presented back to the retailers who see the numbers do not match their own internal reports. They get frustrated and this leads to a problematic relationship. The other challenge is that retailers often restate their data and the KAM's will often not notice the changes in numbers or do not have the time to change their reports. This once again exacerbates the situation and causes all sorts of problems during meetings.

Brands also miss out on the opportunity to collate all these different forms of data and turn it into one database. Doing this produces so much value.

If you are a global brand and you are not leveraging every source of data and making it work for you, you are going to have a problem.

At One Red Kite we specialise in turning lots of different data formats into a nice, clean, accurate, easy to use reports and dashboards. We manage all the coding and we automatically spot changes in data and restates. We then build dashboards to help our clients maximise their data and create internal efficiencies within our clients businesses. Everything just works. As for accuracy? Well… We have a unique approach that ensures you have the most accurate data available. We also work with our clients to code the data so that they can compare a single products performance across the world. I have taken my retailer knowledge and applied it to the data that brands receive and help them make the most out of it.

Imagine the impact clean, accurate data can have on your business.

During COVID, the smart brands continued to work on their data. For them, they needed to know which retailers, regions and companies were coming back online and selling again. It allowed them to react and respond faster. This meant that they could reallocate their resources in the most efficient way to maximise every opportunity.

One Red Kite acts like a part of our client's business. We are essentially an extension of their teams and so this creates a trusting relationship that delivers value. Outsourcing to us really does take tasks away and frees up KAM's to be doing the things that will add value to their business.

Of course, other options are available. The KAM's can continue to work on the data and not be selling or building relationships. Another option is the use of interns. The problem here is that interns change regularly and there is a lack of consistency in terms of accuracy and methodology. The desire is always to work WITH the data and analyse it rather than do the laborious task of cleaning, coding and checking the data.

One final option that I will touch on is automation. There are software options that claim to clean the data you have automatically. Once the data format is set up in theory when you drop a new data file into the folder the software automatically extracts the data and creates a file with the output. Unfortunately, Travel Retail data does not lend itself to this approach. File formats can change, labelling can change, number types (is it units, cases or sales value?) can change from month to month. This leads to huge problems for the brands. The lure of "automation" and "cheap" comes at an expense. This usually ends up with the brand client checking the data and sending it back to their service provider until it is clean and accurate. We have seen brands go through this cycle 4 or 5 times in a month and the data will still be inaccurate. For now, automated processing is not reliable or cost effective when you take into consideration the level of checking, returning and re-checking that is involved. At least our clients have confidence in the data they have and we can prove why that data is accurate.

All of these approaches erode trust in the numbers within businesses. Starting to see a picture of why data is an issue? Can you relate to some of these issues and concerns?

In short, data becomes the hot potato that brands often do not want to spend money on processing and cleaning but it is the very thing that will add value to any business. If you know what has been happening and you can evaluate changes in performances, then you can make better decisions about future actions. Using accurate data in the right way you can:

- Evaluate sales performances
- Review the effect on changes in prices (using average price paid)
- Evaluate promotions and activations
- Establish the impact of competitor activity on your sales
- Understand the impact of marketing
- Combine the data with passenger numbers to establish Spend Per Head
- Use it to create budgets and forecast sales
- Calculate vendor rebates quickly and accurately

- Create centralised decisions to ensure resources are deployed in the right place at the right time
- Spot new trends and act accordingly
- Create business cases to establish the Return on Investment
- Overlay currency exchange rates to see the impact on performance

When you can see that there is so much that can be done with good data, it is worth investing a little to make sure that the data you do have is correct.

So why is data so difficult to come by?

Within the domestic market, data is readily available. In Travel Retail, category data is a little more difficult to get and for good reason. If a retailer wins an airport for a 5 year contract, there is a risk that they could lose it at the end of the 5 years to another player. If category data were to get into the wrong hands, a competitor could do some business modelling to create a winning proposal the next time the location came up for tender. This is the real reason retailers are precious about their data. Within the domestic market, a competitor isn't going to pull the rug from under you and steal your site. They might open up just down the road but, given the nature of airport retail, competitors are not going to be entering your airport.

The highly protective nature of our channel makes it difficult to understand the bigger picture. Brands need to rely on great relationships and a healthy dose of trust to open up a dialogue to get more data than just their own sales.

There have been a number of providers that have tried to solve this puzzle over the years but there has always been the question of accuracy, dubious modelling and forecasts that have led to failed attempts. At the time of writing, there is an attempt to do this with Confectionery but I already foresee a number of pitfalls given my

Travel Retailer background. Time will tell if this works out. For now, I believe that there is another way but, as you might expect, I am keeping this one out of the book!

So, with such protectionist approaches to data the only thing left is for brands to squeeze as much value out of the data they receive. A number of conversations with clients and potential clients has highlighted that there is a fair amount of "Dark Data" sat on servers and hard drives around the world. Dark Data is data that has value but is not being used. Data likes to play with other forms of data to create a rich tapestry or story of what is happening in the world around us. We have been helping our clients create comprehensive reports and dashboards for years to enable our clients to have a competitive edge. I would urge any brand or retailer to complete a "Dark Data Audit" and start to drive some real value from it to give you an advantage over your competitors and drive incremental growth.

So, back to my point. Test and Measure.

Once you have your data in a great place, it really is important to start and continue gathering a record of the activities you have been undertaking. You need to highlight the following:

- What you have done
- Where you have done it
- When it was done

We then advise that this is coded and added to the sales data. This makes it easier for you and your teams to analyse the activities to see which one's deliver better results. If approached in the right way and with appropriate time taken to prepare your data properly (yes this can be a time consuming task but most definitely worth the effort as you will only need to do it once) you can use pivot tables in Excel to analyse multiple activities at the same time. This makes the process of analysis faster, more reliable and more consistent.

Each category, brand and data tend to be different and so I will not share the specific steps to combining an activity planner with sales data but my team can certainly help you if ever the need arose.

Now that you have your activities covered, it is worth considering the smaller and more adhoc changes. Imagine for a moment that you move your products around or you re-angle a fixture or you try some new signage. It is worth considering tracking these changes and doing a piece of adhoc analysis. The aim should be to create a single page of analysis that tells the story. The key headings on the one pager should be as follows:

- Title
- Date & Author
- Assumptions (use bullet points)
- Conclusion / Key Findings (aim for a maximum of 5 bullet points)
- Recommendations (use bullet points where possible)
- Workings Summary (keep this top line)

People are busy and do not want to be wading through pages and pages of a report or analysis. Give them what they need in a short and concise format. Have additional workings in a file somewhere but for now, give them the top line view.

My philosophy is that if someone is going to a meeting to talk about an activity, they are not going to have time to go into the depths of a report. Also, the audiences capacity to remember facts will be limited. This is the reason why I have recommended a maximum of 5 bullet points. This, I have found, has been the most effective way of transferring knowledge in a way that creates action.

As time goes on, with data in a good place, your activities captured and the routine of creating one pagers well practiced, testing and measuring becomes a simple concept to follow and deploy. The collective learning within the organisation will be catapulted and this will lead to better decisions in the future.

What are you waiting for? Begin today!

Utilise Basket Analysis

Mine it, Package It, Sell It

Right now, the forward-thinking brands are screaming out for quality data. Basket data is incredibly powerful and sharing that data can seem like a huge threat to the retailer. There are ways to mine it (to find insights), package the data up into easy-to-use dashboards and to sell access to it.

Imagine this for a moment – Eva is a brand ambassador. She starts her shift at the airport. She picks up an iPad and scans the data for the day ahead. She can see that there are some key China flights leaving today. The reporting tool tells her:

- Which of her brands the Chinese prefer
- How much they typically spend
- How many units they have in the average basket
- The difference in purchasing behaviour between those travelling to Shanghai and Beijing
- Which other categories that the Chinese passenger are likely to buy
- It recommends bolt on products to build their basket
- It shows how many transactions there are likely to be

Armed with this information, Eva walks onto the shop floor and makes sure that her section is set up to a high standard. She looks at her watch and see's that the Chinese passengers will be arriving soon and so she turns the show cards round so that the Cantonese text is showing on her promotion. She is ready to maximise every sale. She knows what to recommend instead of trying to sell to them. Eva has the inside track.

This sounds too good to be true but we have and continue to develop this kind of software. The limitation rests with the retailer as sharing these types of reports and insights are sometimes seen as giving too much away.

This is something that retailers could sell, however. The data could be shared in a way that does not give away the 'big picture' and does not enable individual brands to calculate the total sales. This therefore presents value to the user and a financial gain for the retailer both through a subscription service and through increased sales. Destination targeting has been proved to be a powerful tool to improve sales and conversion.

Optimise Performance Through Better Targeting

By utilising basket data, retailers can better target key destinations, nationalities (if that data is captured at the point of sale) and carriers. If you can see that sales to Destination X vary depending on the carrier, you can run some analysis to work out why there is a difference in sales. If Carrier A's sales are typically 10% more than Carrier B, a campaign to target those travelling on Carrier B can be deployed to deliver an increase in sales of +10%. When looking at basket sales according to destination and carrier, you can seek out imbalances and opportunities to find growth. Seek out the "biggest prizes" first, these opportunities will generate the best returns if delivered.

Utilising such data will ensure that you can deploy the right resources at the right place and time. This will help with sales, staff management, agency deployment, queue management and more.

Better Research

One thing to also consider is that basket data can lead to better research. Right now, research can be too generalised and varies significantly from what retailers are seeing in store (a number of brands have approached us with this feedback and have asked us to recommend alternative research companies). By identifying which flights are the key spending flights, research teams can be deployed near the gates for those flights. While people are sat waiting to board, research staff can speak to individuals. Alternatively, the till staff can ask shoppers on those target flights if they would like to complete a survey and refer them to the researcher.

This approach leads to better quality data that can be used to generate insights. To supercharge this further, contact us for more details. We can't give away all of our secrets!

Retailers should consider creating their own research teams to sell value adding research to brands. This drives innovation and learning. The research would be a validated and trusted source of insight that the retailers have confidence in and therefore the brands too can trust it.

Become An Insight Business That Sells Products

In summary, retailers should be working towards becoming an insight business that also sells products. There is a huge amount that retailers could be doing to learn more about the behaviour and preferences of different nationalities and destinations. This is something that brands in both travel and domestic retail would be interested to learn more about.

Use Space Planning as a Catalyst

A significant portion of this book has been handed over to Space Planning and for good reason. It is the one area within retail that is not consistent across the industry. Some retailers have a space planning function, some do not. Some brands create planograms, some have merchandising rules.

The Small Cog That Aligns Everything

If approached in the right way, space planning is a cross functional department that can really help you coordinate large parts of the retail business. It can:

- Help you control the range / assortment size
- Provide Marketing information on POS sizes / lightbox sizes etc
- Help make space work harder
- Create consistency and maintain store standards
- Support effective evaluation of space changes and activations

Tighter Controls

One thing about retail is that it can create a life of its own. I remember when I first joined WDF, the store managers had control over the range and invariably, you would find product that was in the stock room because there was no space on the shelves. You would end up with gaps because the fastest moving lines did not have enough stock on shelf. In short, for that approach to work, you would need rubber fixtures.

By taking back control, limiting the range and having a strict one in, one out policy, stores can create a sense of focus. Products have space to breath and service the shopper appropriately.

Evaluate, Evaluate, Evaluate

I cannot stress this enough. I have mentioned it before – test and measure! As with all other parts of the business, Space Planning needs to become a learning function. Try things, test it, measure it and decide whether something has worked on not. If it has, think about how the learnings can be applied to the wider estate.

If you are a retailer, you might consider handing over one store as a test site. It can become a playground for the entire business to run trials and see how things work. Put up CCTV cameras, capture footage and see how shoppers interact with the product, the fixture, the department and the store. Yes, it may seem like a big brother production but it will help revolutionise the channel massively. Shoppers often cannot tell you why they do things or they may even post rationalise it. Some research companies are asking people about their purchases up to 6 months after the event. I can barely remember what I ate last Friday never mind what I bought in an airport 6 months ago.

By observing them in action, you can really create some amazing insights. I have learned so much by just sitting outside stores and watching how people interact. It has meant that I have made better recommendations for clients.

Space Planning can be at the forefront of store transformations and shopper research because it is a function that must interact with most other functions to ensure that everything runs smoothly.

Whatever you do, make sure you evaluate the changes you make and learn from them.

Merchandising

Merchandising relates to how the product shows up in store. If a store does not have a Macro and Micro Space Planning function, the retailer can provide guidelines as to how products should show up on displays.

Good, Better, Best

The most common principle is the Good, Better, Best principle. This is where you group products in terms of quality as seen below. In Option 1 we see Good on the bottom 2 shelves, the next one up is Better and the top shelf is Best. This means that the lowest price products are on the bottom and the higher priced products at the top.

One slight variation to this can be seen in Option 2 and this is where Better is at the Top and Best is on the second shelf down. This is due to the old saying that the "Eye Line Is The Buy Line". What this tries to do is to focus the shopper on the highest price products. In some categories, shelf positioning can make all the difference in terms of sales.

Which one is right? This can vary by category and the height of the fixture and so experimentation is required. As is the mantra throughout this book – "Test & Measure".

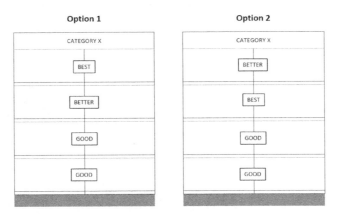

In some locations (if certain criteria is met) it may be useful to experiment with different products varying by margin to maximise purchasing and profitability. In this scenario "Good Better Best" relates to levels of margin.

Merchandising Standards

All the usual factors with regards to merchandising standards should be adhered to. These include:

- Clean shelves
- Stock pulled forward
- Tickets in place
- Lightboxes working
- Fixtures in good repair
- Signage is correct
- Empty spaces have been filled
- Till points are tidy and ready to open
- Till point products are replenished and ready to go

All of the above are what you would expect in store however this is rarely the case.

Other factors surrounding merchandising may include include:

- Minimum Facings
- Keeping Brand Families Together
- Following A Price Logic
- Colour Blocking
- Alphabetical Merchandising

Minimum facings

To have a credible offer and one that can be easily shopped, it is important to ensure that you have enough facings of any particular product. This might mean having a minimum of 2 or 3 facings, regardless of how well it sells. Super premium products will be different – 3 facings of a £5,000 product is probably going to tie up cash in stock that is unlikely to sell through in 12 months maybe longer.

Whatever you follow, ensure that you are consistent across the subcategory. Whiskies may end up with single facings if it is for a specialist store which niche products.

As a rule, It is recommended that a minimum of 2 facings are applied.

Keeping Brand Families Together

Once again, this is something that will require testing and experimentation. In some categories, it makes sense to keep brand families (all the sub brands of a parent brand) together. This is sometimes called Brand Blocking. This is key when a brand is a destination product and you want to encourage trade up within said brand. Examples might be when you have 12 year old, 15, year old, 18 year old etc. Whiskies under the same parent brand and you want to encourage trade up from a brand loyal shopper.

There is an argument to split the products and group them by their type. In this situation you would put all the 12-year-olds together, then all of the 15 year olds and so forth.

Which is correct? This can vary by category and different options should be tested and evaluated. Whatever the final decision, be consistent. In the first instance, try to keep the brand families together.

Follow A Price logic

There is nothing more frustrating than looking at a display and not being able to easily find a product in the price range you want to buy it in. Keeping products in price order is a good idea even if you are brand blocking or Colour Blocking.

Price logic should always be highest price earliest in the customer flow, lowest price at the end of the flow. The premise here is that is easier for the shopper to start high and work their way down than it is to get people to trade up.

In the diagram below, you have customer flowing left to right and so the highest price is in the top left hand corner.

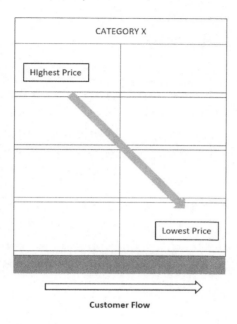

CATEGORY X

Highest Price

Lowest Price

Customer Flow

Colour Blocking

Some space planners and visual merchandisers believe that products should be grouped and merchandised according to the colour of the packaging. Whilst this may be visually appealing in some ways, it is rarely logical for the shopper. Colour blocking may have its uses when subcategories have inherent colour differences such as Tequila and Rum. Blocking similar colours together may make sense.

Alphabetical Merchandising

Alphabetical merchandising is where you put products in order based on their position in the alphabet. Great for books where you usually search based on an author's name, not so great if you are merchandising a Duty-Free store. Within these stores, unless you have a subcategory where the shoppers decision tree starts with the name (i.e. an author), it is not advisable to go down this route. Sephora have been known to merchandise by alphabet within Fragrances, its validity in the airport environment is yet to be tested.

Stock Holding & Rate Of Sale

Effective stock management is critical in Travel Retail, particularly in high traffic locations where shelves can be bare in a matter of hours. Out of stock on the shop floor means lost sales. Regular monitoring of Minimum Display Quantities (MDQ's) compared to Rate of Sale (unit sales) will ensure that Out Of Stocks (OOS) are kept to a minimum.

Another thing to remember is that a product may make it out to store but it can be lost in the stock room. If a product isn't on shelf, how can the shopper buy it? Planograms enable you to have greater control over the store assortment. If lines are sent to the store, they should be on the planogram.

Serve Who You Have

This might seem like common sense however, due to the increasing number of Chinese passengers, retailers and brands have shifted their focus to serve their needs. This has almost been to the exclusion of all other passenger groups. This opens the retailer and brands up to missed opportunities and therefore lost sales.

The Loss of Chinese Passengers

At the time of writing (2022), the Chinese Government were pursuing what appears to be a zero covid strategy. This has led to many restrictions in terms of air travel which, in turn, leads to to significantly lower passenger numbers, which has had a significant impact on sales. The Chinese are known for their spending on super premium products.

Although this view may be controversial, it is actually a good thing that the Chinese are not travelling. It forces retailers to think about the next segment of Commercially Important Passengers (CIP's). Commercially Important Passengers tend to be passengers that fly to certain destinations or even to certain cities that have a tendency to spend more than the average. This might be in the form of better Conversion, better Average Transaction Values or both.

Chinese passengers should not be the whole cake, they should be the icing on the cake!

Refocus On The People Travelling Through Your Airport

Covid-19 and the subsequent recovery should have taught Travel Retail about the need for a broad perspective when targeting shoppers. Passenger spend behaviour has changed however, as to whether this remains, time will tell. Experience tells us that those who are the first to travel since Covid have the financial means and stronger intent / need to travel. These people are likely to have more disposable income and will therefore spend more in stores. As the passenger numbers increase, it is likely that those with lower levels of disposable income will begin to travel and therefore spending will fall back in line and return to pre-covid levels. One caveat on this however is that price increases (due to inflation) are likely to be the driver of growth vs pre-pandemic times.

In the UK there is a saying – "Make hay while the sun shines". This means that it is more important than ever for Travel Retail to maximise every opportunity. Lamenting over the loss of Chinese passengers will not change anything. If you are a retailer:

- Review your data
- Identify target opportunities in the form of Destinations and Nationalities
- Adapt your assortment, space and promotions
- Execute and monitor

Keep this cycle going regularly (probably every 2 months) to ensure that every opportunity is taken.

Brilliant Basics

In retail, it is common to want to go after the shiny new ideas and approaches however, like anything, this must be built on a solid foundation. A solid foundation is built on the ability to execute the basics well.

In a session with Liz Abram (ex-military interrogator who worked on the TV show SAS Who Dares Wins), I asked her what makes the SAS so good at what they do. Her view was that it is easy to get lost in some of the amazing things that they achieve but it all boils down to one simple idea. They are BRILLIANT (and I mean next level brilliant) at the basics. The basics is something that is never left behind. Once you know how to do the basics, most move on to bigger and better things. The very best continue to practice, practice, practice.

In reality does this happen in Retail? No. Not in Travel Retail or Domestic. In fact, it is not uncommon for domestic retailers to have Merchandising teams who freshen up a store and bring it back up to opening store standards. There is another saying, God and The Devil are in the detail. This is absolutely true in all forms of retail.

How To Build The SAS Of Retail

To build a truly elite retail team there are some strict requirements that must be followed. Retailers need to look to the likes of hotels such as Claridges and Corinthia to really understand the level of detail that should be strived for. To achieve this, the following is essential:

- **The Right People**
  Employ people who are passionate about serving others, delivering a quality experience and focused on high

standards. The team should have pride in what they are doing and will be highly motivated to keep their sections maintained to the highest standards. These people need to be attentive to the shoppers needs, have a curiosity to uncover the shopper needs and match the appropriate products to meet those needs.

- **Ever Present SFM's**
  Motivation doesn't last for ever. Having highly visible Sales Floor Managers who are constantly circling the stores, encouraging staff to talk to shoppers, reviewing store standards, acknowledging shoppers and driving performance are essential. Our mystery shopping team rarely catch sight of these managers or team leaders. Teams are often left to get on with running the shop floor and this leads to a decline in standards, motivation and sales.

- **Focus on Store Standards**
  If you are going to achieve "Brilliant Basics", you are going to have to focus on the very finest of details in store. There is no time for staff to chat. There is the age old saying crops up again – "If you can lean you can clean" meaning if you have time to relax and chat, you have time to clean shelves, face up products, sort out tickets etc.

- **Correct Merchandising**
  It is important that the instore execution of promotions and activations are carried out correctly. It is also essential to follow any Planograms that have been created. A lot of work goes into preparing these communications. Failure to plan leads to misleading results and misleading results leads to poor decision making.

- **Right Processes**
  It is really important to ensure that the right processes are put in place. Whether you are a retailer, a brand or an agency,

it is essential to have simple processes to adhere to. This can range from how stores are opened through to how shoppers are approached and interacted with. The use of these processes ensure standardisation which in turn leads to increased efficiency and effectiveness.

Processes will vary by location and so it is important to take time to review the processes on a 6 month basis to check whether the process is still fit for purpose. As discussed in the Diamond Model section, there are always marginal gains that can be achieved. Utilise the team to get their input on how best to improve what you do.

Whatever the process, ensure that it becomes distilled into the simplest form to avoid deviation or prevent bad habits creeping in. This level of clarity makes it easy for teams to understand what is expected of them and therefore what they are measured on.

- **Practice, Practice, Practice**

  Practice takes discipline, it takes routine and a desire to be the best at what you do. There are a number of ways practice can help. One example is handling difficult conversations. This might be with a colleague or a customer. Role playing dealing with a difficult customer enables you to practice, critically review performance in a safe space, review options for improvement and try again. Role playing can often feel uncomfortable but this discomfort works in your favour. It helps you create a library of experience that will help you in future difficult situations.

- **Create A Sense Of Pride**

  If the team is given responsibility and is made accountable, they will experience a sense of pride when things go well. High standards takes continuous hard work but it becomes easier if you take pride in work done well.

In essence, these points are all about breaking down every part of the business and refining it and its capabilities to always be moving forward, to improve and to be the best possible version of itself in any situation. Retail is detail and so it is worth getting those details right.

If you think that your instore execution is on point, think again. Our mystery shopping team have yet to find a highly effective front line experience where there are no opportunities to improve.

Deep Understanding of Promotions and Space

Every year, retailers deploy hundreds of promotions in store. Some work, some see no changes in performance, others fail but all of this goes largely unnoticed. As long as sales appear to be going up, little is done to deeply understand the effect of promotions on the products themselves or the category they sit within.

Detailed analysis can uncover what works well and what doesn't. It is in the interest of retailers and brands to identify:

- Which mechanics work?
- Which brands do they work on?
- Which stores did the promotions work in?
- Did the store have the right amount of stock?
- Was the promotion in a good location in store?
- Was the promotion supported with the right staff and staffing levels?
- Which destinations (or nationalities) are buying?
- How has the promotion impacted the category?
- Has the promotion cannibalised sales or grown the category?
- Why does it work?
- Who benefited the most from the promotion?

- Did the promotion increase profitability for both the retailer and the brand?
- What would you do differently?
- Who has the advantage? The retailer or the brand?

Why is all of this important? Well, brands that can answer all or most of these questions can utilise all of these learnings to negotiate better terms with the retailer.

Don't just look at the promotion from your perspective, look at it from the other side too.

If you work for a brand and you are evaluating the promotions, go beyond evaluating from your own perspective. You have all of the information you need from your sell out data and your trade terms and agreements. You will know the average selling price, the cost price that you are providing and so you can calculate the cash margins that the retailer is achieving. This can be compared to the value that you derive from the promotion too. If you see that your promotion has broken even for your brand but you calculate that the retailer gained $100k through selling the space, additional staffing, better cost prices, listing fees and increased sales, maybe it is time to review your negotiations for next time.

Another reason why it is important to invest time into understanding promotions is because it can often seem like you are doing well but this is not always the case. Most brands do not factor seasonality into the equation. Based in the usual cycle of sales, promotions can often be a result of circumstance (i.e. seasonal uplift in passenger numbers) rather than doing a better job at converting shoppers.

Remember, Promotions are Linked to Space

If you are a brand, it makes sense to consider where your promotions are within the store. Each time you experience a change in location, capture that change and evaluate it. It can make a huge difference. A weak promotion in a 'hot spot' is likely to perform better than a strong promotion in a 'cold spot'. The best approach to this would be as follows:

- Set up a 3 year tracking study
- Select up to 5 key airport locations where promotions and activations are run
- Monitor the location of the execution in store
- Track performance pre promotion vs promotion
- Keep a file that shows the history of the changes over time and their performance
- Utilise this data to enable deeper conversations with the retailer to drive for better outcomes
- Sharpen your promotional executions and mechanics based on the performances

For those brands who are super keen on understanding their performances, it is worth tracking the other brands that go onto those promotional sites and activation sites. What happens to your sales when competitors go on promotion, what is the impact of that in terms of cash sales for your brand? It isn't easy to do but it is definitely worth investing the time and effort. Do it right and you can utilise your findings to negotiate better space, better position and better trade terms.

If you are a retailer, track the changes in sales each time a promotional site changes. In a recent study we found that a particular promotional site was best suited to Confectionery rather than Liquor. Further investigation showed the reason for this was due to the path the shopper took to the till points. Other locations within the store were better suited to other categories. Having this detailed understanding of which sites work well for each subcategory can lead to significant insights and increased cross category performances.

One final point to make regarding space and promotions is to monitor stock levels. Insufficient space will lead to low stock which will therefore impact sales. By using the tracking techniques mentioned above, you can start to improve predictions for stock requirements to satisfy demand and customer needs. This can lead to better activation design, better space selection and an improved experience for the shopper... Meaning more sales!

To summarise, so much effort goes into promotions, it would make sense to ensure that you have total understanding of what works, where it works and why.

PART
10

SUMMARY

Well, you have stuck with it this far so thank you!

The key takeaways from this book have been as follows:

- Walk a mile in the retailers' shoes and really understand the day to day challenges that they operate under.
- Remember the key stages of the shopper journey
  - Pre-Airport
  - Arriving
  - Check in
  - Security
  - Departures
- Consider the touch points and potential micro fails that impact propensity to spend
- Know the retailer metrics
  - Think differently about performance
    - Think Conversion
    - Think Units Per Basket
    - Think Average Price
    - Think Pax
    - Think Spend Per Head
  - Speak their language (use their terminology)
- Develop basket analysis capability
- Bring in Category Management Principles

- - Target shopper missions and reasons for purchasing
  - Create an appropriate range
  - Implement Space Planning
    - It doesn't need to be complex
    - Macro space can be enough to evaluate performance & efficiency
- Remember AIDA
- Segment & target your shoppers and locations appropriately
- Remember that not one size fits all
- Evaluate promotions & activations
- Obsess about the detail
- Strive for better
  - Better relationships
  - Change our reality
  - Focus on service
  - Use the diamond model

Travel retail is such a vast subject but I have tried to capture all the aspects that are transferrable across the channel. The biggest challenge I see is the gap between what retailers know and what brands believe. This can improve through better dialogue and better understanding.

If you are a brand, you can make huge leaps forward by following these 5 steps.

- **Stop** – Put your agenda on hold
- **Listen** – Really listen to what the retailer is saying
- **Understand** – Check that you understand their situation completely
- **Align** – Think about how you can align your needs with theirs
- **Suggest** – Show the retailer how your solutions will help solve their challenges

When dealing with retailers in Travel Retail, less really is more. Step into THEIR reality, step into what is important to them, the challenges they face. Leave your goals and agenda at the door and seek to build trust first. This might seem counter intuitive however, because this is a relatively rare thing, it will actually pay dividends in the end.

A FINAL WORD

Finally, I wish you every success in your career within Travel Retail. I hope this book offers you some help and guidance on your path. If you have found this helpful or you have some suggestions, do drop me a line at kevin.brocklebank@oneredkite.com.

If One Red Kite (www.oneredkite.com) can support you business with any of the topics covered in this book, please do drop me a line.

Printed in Great Britain
by Amazon

28978675R00175